12 CONVERSATIONS TO CHANGE
YOUR CHILD'S FINANCIAL FUTURE

It
Makes
Total
Cents

TOM HENSKE, CFP®

It Makes Total Cents: 12 Conversations to Change Your Child's Financial Future

For information about this title or to order other books and/or electronic media, contact the publisher:
Total Cents, LLC
Tom Henske
606 Post Road East, Suite 702
Westport, CT 06880
www.totalcents.com
tom@totalcents.com

ISBN: 979-8-9862832-0-3 (print)
        979-8-9862832-1-0 (eBook)

Printed in the United States of America

The information provided in this book is for educational purposes only. It is not intended to be a source of financial or legal advice. Making adjustments to a financial strategy or plan should only be undertaken after consulting with a professional. The publisher and the author make no guarantee of financial results obtained by using this book.

CRN202806-2569188

Securities and investment advisory services offered through qualified registered representatives of MML Investors Services, LLC, Member SIPC. (90 Park Avenue, New York, NY 10016, 212-536-6000)

DEDICATION

For my wife, Stacey, for being my partner in educating our kids and so much else in life,

for our children, Spencer and Samantha, for being receptive to learning

and for my parents, Tom and Jerri, who never made money a taboo topic in our home.

Acknowledgments

WHEN I EMBARKED ON THE project of putting my twenty-seven-plus years of studying the how-to of financial education, I never imagined how many people were going to help me along the way.

Thanks to my wife, Stacey, for endeavoring to develop money smarts in our own children which served as a petri dish for what I've written here. We learned a ton together about what to do, and more important, what not to do. This has been a family affair and my children, Spencer and Samantha, have been tremendous resources—from letting me practice on them, to designing our brand, to being brave enough to tell me when I was doing it wrong.

I now have a better appreciation for my own parents, Tom and Jerri, who I realized were amazing at how they taught me about money and didn't make money a taboo topic in our house growing up. They, too, encouraged me to drive this project forward to help other families.

There were tons of friends who helped me on this specific financial literacy project along the way including (in alphabetical order, not playing favorites!): Ben Arthur, Stuart Barefoot, Caroline Barney, Jen Callen Beveridge, David Colen, Roger Crandall, Josh Dick, Darren Feeney, Courtney Ferrell, Peter Haines, Noah Hendler, Jared Herman, Amy Kunihiro, Terrance McMahon, Ruth Moskowitz, Jim Pavia, Jodi Ross, Jennifer Rutley, Linda Skidmore, SRH Design, Paula Tremblay, Pete

Trizzino, Eric Schwartzman, The UVA IMP Society, Gretchen Tibbits, John Vacarro, Ross Weiner, and Dan Woog.

I wouldn't be at the point where I could kick off this endeavor if it weren't for unbelievable professionals such as my book architect, Stuart Horwitz; my web and social media experts at The Snyder Group; all the folks at the Westport Library's Verso Studio (Travis Bell, you're going to heaven for having to deal with me on those podcasts); and many others.

And last, but not least, there were some titans of the financial literacy space who were rooting me on along the way: Thanks to Joline Godfrey, my guru on the topic, for inspiring me 20 years ago and keeping me going. I can't forget John Lanza, who took my call and met me while he was on vacation with his daughter, and challenged me to think deeper on these topics. There was also Don McPherson, who 99.9% of people in the USA think of as a legendary college football player and Heisman finalist—but to me he'll always be the champion of how the kids of today learn.

TABLE OF CONTENTS

Introduction   1

Lesson One: Get Money Into Their Hands   13

Lesson Two: Teach Them the Value of a Dollar   25

Lesson Three: Show Them How to Budget   33

Lesson Four: Encourage Them to Save   37

Lesson Five: Educate Them on Compound Interest   45

Lesson Six: Expose Them to Investing   51

Lesson Seven: Break the News About Taxes   59

Lesson Eight: Explain Borrowing and Credit   67

Lesson Nine: Inspire Them to be Charitable   75

Lesson Ten: Advise Them About Insurance   81

Lesson Eleven: Demystify Legal Documents   91

Lesson Twelve: Warn Them About Money Safety   101

Conclusion   111

INTRODUCTION

I'VE BEEN A FINANCIAL ADVISOR for nearly three decades. Over that time, I have gathered too many professional designations to name, resulting in Tom Henske being followed by the acronyms CFP®, CLU, CTS, CHFC, CFS, CES, and CLTC.

However, on the topic of teaching your kids about money, I have two better qualifications. I've been a parent for 18 years and a varsity high school soccer coach for 11 years. That means I understand how kids think, learn, and what language to use as we try to educate them.

There is a proverb that instructs: "If you want to know about the road ahead, ask the person coming back." That's me—I've been down this road before, dozens of times, and I've watched other parents who have been down this road too. I've learned, by trial and error, what money topics are important to teach, when and how to teach them.

Throughout my 27 years of advising, I have seen a fair number of clients come into my office for financial advice who exhibited similar patterns. In a large number of cases these anxious and overwhelmed clients attributed their stress to not developing good money habits early in their lives. Small problems in their young adulthood got bigger later on in their lives.

In one case, a client shared his history of health problems over the years which he attributed to the dysfunctional relationship he had with his personal finances. After his latest heart problem, his doctor advised him to reduce the stress in his life. At age 50, he decided his biggest stressor was money and knew he needed to finally get his financial life in order. In the meantime, his lack of money skills led to stress that damaged his marriage (he was a spender...his wife a saver), strained the relationship with his own parents when he asked them to bail him out, and turned into a constant battle with his kids who he said "thought money grew on trees."

That leads me to ask you a question:

> Would you ever intentionally put your child at risk of having a stressful life that leads to poor health, broken relationships, and potential substance-abuse problems?

No parent would purposely do that to their children. Yet, you might unconsciously be on that path, if you are not prioritizing having talks with your kids about money, before it is too late.

And not only is this stress bad for your physical and emotional well-being—but also it is bad for your mental well-being too. We have all heard stories of seemingly good people making bad choices when hit by financial stress. Under stress, blood flow is reduced to those parts of the brain that excel in problem-solving, concentration, planning, and impulse control.

How can we avoid putting our kids in situations where this stress takes over? How do we help them stay clear about their goals and the actions that are benefiting those goals? We must educate them about money, pure and simple.

The thing is, your kids will learn about money at some point. The questions are: from who and when? In a perfect world, we as parents would pool our knowledge and resources on this topic to make sure our children have a foundational knowledge about money that will help them thrive and prevent potential problems in their future.

In the world we live in, however, it is up to you. Parents are responsible for the development of their children's financial literacy. If you don't take ownership of that role in your child's development, you know who is waiting in the wings to do it for you? That's right, you guessed it: social media. More on this in a bit.

THE WAY THIS BOOK WORKS

A picture is worth a thousand words here. This is the formula I'd like you to follow:

How It Works			
Read Chapter	**Listen to Podcast**	**Send TikTok**	**Dinner Conversation**
Read one chapter per month (15 minutes)	Listen to the corresponding podcast episode (10 minutes)	Send your child the lesson's TikTok Intro (1 minute)	Ask them a few questions at dinner (20 minutes)

This is all I'm going to ask of you as a parent—46 minutes a month. And I'll ask even less of your child—21 minutes if I'm doing my math correctly. That will not add tremendously to your workload or theirs. And, it's crucial for your child's future.

STEP 1: READ THE NEXT LESSON IN THIS BOOK

Do not read past the next lesson. You don't need to. Save your energy. Let's not make this a bigger or more daunting project than it needs to be.

STEP 2: LISTEN TO THE CORRESPONDING PODCAST EPISODE

For the first 10 minutes each month, you (the parent) are going to listen to my podcast which sets up the conversation you will have with your kids. These podcasts will be quick (I'm not exaggerating when I say each episode is about 10 minutes in length), entertaining, easy to understand, and lifesaving for your children. I am going to teach you, the parent, how to bring up certain money topics at home with your kids—how to start these conversations.

In 10 minutes, how can I become an expert, you might say? You won't. You are not trying to be the money guru. I am giving you four or five questions to ask which will keep the conversation going while I outline the likely responses your kids will have. I've tried this in my own home; the questions are field-tested and good to go.

STEP 3: SEND YOUR CHILD THE LESSON'S TIKTOK INTRO

Have you heard of TikTok? This social media platform is all the rage with teenagers. TikTok hosts a variety of short-form user videos, from genres like pranks, jokes, and dances with durations ranging from a few seconds to three minutes.

You will forward your child a one-minute TikTok (which I will provide) to watch. And then you're going to talk about one topic a month as your dinnertime conversation.

STEP 4: HAVE THE DINNER CONVERSATION

While this feels like the hard part, it's actually pretty easy. You'll bring the list of four or five questions from the podcast, which I'll also make available with a single-page sheet in case you listen to podcasts in the car or while on the cardio machine. In our house, we like to make it special by making the kids' favorite meal or ordering pizza on the nights we are having the money conversation.

You throw the questions out there and let them talk. Your goal is just to broaden their awareness of personal finance and more important, to remove the taboo of talking about money. Plain and simple.

ONLY AT DINNER?

Don't get caught up on whether or not dinner is the right time for these conversations. You can easily substitute long walks, car drives to practices, or even sitting at a local coffee shop for the concept to work. For the sake of ease, I am going to use the word "dinnertime" and you can mentally substitute your favorite venue every time I say that.

As a side note, I do really like dinnertime for these conversations in my own house. Why?

The pandemic reminded us of the tremendous value of having dinner together as a family. Here are a few of the reasons why:

- Eating together improves family relationships, fosters a sense of stability, belonging, and connectedness.
- Mealtime conversations have been tied to improved literacy. Dinner time conversations increase a child's vocabulary.[1, 2]
- And my favorite quote: "Experts say the magic of sit-down mealtime happens when families gather to talk, laugh, share their day-to-day struggles, and support each other through life's ups and downs. These moments of connection nurture a sense of belonging, leading to greater self-esteem and self-confidence."[3]

---

[1] https://blog.erlanger.org/2021/11/23/the-importance-of-family-meal-time/

[2] https://watermark.silverchair.com/peds_20174276.pdf?token=AQECAH i208BE49Ooan9kkhW_Ercy7Dm3ZL_9Cf3qfKAc485ysgAAAuAwggL cBgkqhkiG9w0BBwagggLNMIICyQIBADCCAsIGCSqGSIb3DQEH ATAeBglghkgBZQMEAS4wEQQMSLBDvDWBHpOSSPynAgEQgI ICk7-SmNR8lTXiZ-m8PVZKX4pNUBcEMHvWll-

[3] https://www.eatingdisorderhope.com/blog/value-sit-down-family-meals-emotional-health

As I mentioned earlier, discussions about money are often conversations about family values. And dinner is a great time to talk about family values. For example, some families don't allow anyone to have their smartphone at the dinner table. That's a family value, isn't it?

In a similar way, these dinnertime conversations will be about more than learning money concepts. You see, how someone manages their finances is really a reflection of their values.

What are values? Values pertain to the family's structure, function, roles, beliefs, attitudes, and ideals. In a general sense, these can be things like:

- Valuing one's elders.
- Hard work.
- Respect.
- Compassion.
- Responsibility.
- Creativity.
- Kindness.

Now, each of those values can be applied to money—once the taboo nature of money is taken off the table. How you feel about money, for better or worse, helps shape the financial decisions you make in your life. Financial planners often say, "Show me someone's checkbook, and I'll be able to tell you what's really important to them."

We're now in a digital age where that saying is obsolete, but the gist is exactly the same if you look at people's online bank statements. People tend to use their money in ways that align with their values, which are reflected in their habits.

Don't Be Afraid to Have These Conversations

Even the thought of having one conversation about money with your kid may trigger you—let alone the twelve conversations I am going to ask you to have over the course of a year. That is largely because our generation grew up with the belief that talking about money was taboo. Can you imagine the reactions of our parents if we would have ever dared to ask a question like:

- How much do you make?
- How much are we worth?
- How much did our house cost?

This left us with a legacy of avoidance. A recent T. Rowe Price survey found approximately 70% of parents had "some reluctance" to discussing money with their children. Many experts are quick to point to this as the reason why we need financial education in our schools. That is probably right, but in our situation, we don't have the time for the education system to get caught up—not for our kids, anyway. Maybe schools will have seen the light in time for our grandkids.

What this means is that we, as parents, are going to have to get comfortable being uncomfortable as we talk about money. My hope is that you'll not only embrace the conversations we're going to have as a family, but also that you and your kids will actually enjoy the topic.

Wait. You Want Us to Put More Social Media In Front Of Our Kids?

Social media can have many positive attributes. However, building financial literacy has not traditionally been one of them. In fact, when

Charles Schwab conducted their Modern Wealth Index Survey, they ended up putting the blame for the development of bad financial habits squarely on the shoulders of social media.

Some of the highlights that Schwab found in this survey and how social media led to disastrous financial futures include:

- **Keeping up with the Joneses.** Today's parents would never publicly admit that the house they live in, the car they drive, the jewelry they wear, and the vacations they take are often influenced by a need to compete with others around them. Overall, competition can be a healthy trait, and it's not one we would try to minimize here. There is a time and place for everything. The competition to try and spend at the rate of another household seems to defy any logic.

  Schwab found that more than one-third of Americans admit that social media has influenced them to spend money on experiences—like the experiences their friends share on social media platforms. This need to keep up with the Joneses, which really boils down to putting too much credence into what others think of you, predates any of our lives and has probably been here since the beginning of time. In modern-day lingo, we might call this FOMO (Fear Of Missing Out). Unfortunately, this need to care about what impresses other people, is leading a whole generation down a road of underfunded retirement. This results in a need to lean on their adult children because they didn't adequately save—and it is now too late to find out that keeping up with the Joneses was not worth it.

- **Spending beyond their means.** A variation on keeping up with the Joneses is reflected in poor budgeting—spending more than you make. The Schwab survey reported that more than one-third of Americans admitted to having spent "more money than they can afford" in order to participate in experiences with their friends. The study ranked social media platforms as the biggest "bad" influence on how respondents manage their money.

Here's the good news. In the study, respondents also rank friends and family as their top "good" influences. That's exactly the point I've been trying to make. The strong influence that you, your child's parent, play in making sure money topics are actually discussed at home can demonstrate how your own family values are reflected in the way you spend. This gives them an up close and personal view of how they should live their own life as it pertains to staying within their budget and not regularly spending more than they make.

- **Focusing on spending over saving.** More than half of survey respondents said they pay more attention to how their friends spend money than to how they save money. It's sad that 60% of respondents said they are at a loss to understand how their friends can afford the vacations and restaurant meals that they post about on social media platforms. We'll tell you why—it's because they are spending too much money and NOT saving.

When was the last time you saw a glut of social media posts touting, "I just put $100 in my bank account." Or, "Yippee for me, I started putting away money into my retirement plan." Not sexy, not social-media worthy, not cool...until one gets to retirement—where "cool" is defined as being financially secure and able to continue your preretirement lifestyle with no insecurity that you'll run out of money. If the end goal is to either never be able to retire, or to run out of money in retirement, then social media may very well be doing all it can to get us there!

But We Can Use Social Media to Help Us

How is that going to happen? Algorithms!

According to recent data by Tallo, 38% of Gen Zers have received financial advice from TikTok, reporting they're likely to turn to the platform to get advice on long- and short-term savings as well as budgeting tips.

That's where we're going to engage with them and then let the system work in our favor. Did you ever notice when you are shopping online for something, let's say a pair of shoes, and then your social media feeds get flooded with posts about shoes, advertisements about shoes, the history of shoes, and pictures of shoes? It's like the internet is listening into your conversations or reading your mind.

Well, in our case, when your kids click on the initial Total Cents TikTok money introduction for that month's financial subject, it is going to kick off a tsunami of similar posts that show up in their feed without you having to do a thing. And now they are learning in their own language—Social Media'ese. If you can't beat them, join them.

The End Result

If you can engage your kids in conversations about money while demonstrating your family's values, the benefits will far exceed making them fiscally responsible. If you stay diligent about bringing these conversations up once a month, your kids are going to build a money vocabulary, and more important, it will open the lines of communication between you and them in a way you might never have experienced.

The result is that you are going to experience amazingly thoughtful and insightful observations and questions from your children. You aren't going to just focus on teaching them about trading stocks—in the future, they might be able to hire a financial advisor for that. You are going to teach them to attach your family values to how they save, spend, invest, and donate to name some of the topics we are going to cover together in this book.

I'm here to help us accomplish this for our kids. Let's get started.

LESSON ONE: GET MONEY INTO THEIR HANDS

Money is best understood by doing, not reading.

ONE OF THE MUST-DO'S TO DEVELOP a financially literate child is to let them practice. Kids have to get real money into their hands to give them context and life experience or all of our dinner conversations will be for naught.

Let me give you this metaphor using one of my favorite subjects, soccer. Imagine your daughter wants to learn to play soccer. Lots of her friends are playing, but she has historically shied away from the sport because she isn't good (yet!) and feels embarrassed to play with other girls who have been playing for a couple of years.

Being the good parent that you are, you pump her up with Speech #37 (you know that one, the "You Can Conquer the World" speech). You played soccer back in middle school, so you are at least qualified to give her the first lesson. You get in the car, drive down to the local high school that has a soccer field, and you both jump out excitedly to get her started on the path to a full 4-year college scholarship. You are both on the field, and you happily say to her, "Okay, get to it!"

She stands there looking at you strangely and politely asks, "Don't we need a soccer ball to practice?"

You reply, "No, that's OK. Just run around and imagine you are kicking a ball. That's just as good."

Now, we both know it's not productive to practice soccer without a ball. When you hear it like that you think, "Duh, who would ever do that?" But if I had to guess, I would say that 90% of households do something very similar when it comes to teaching their own kids about money. Then we wonder why kids go to college lacking budgeting skills and why some even build up credit card debt. That happens because they never got to practice with a soccer ball—real money in their hands—and had to figure out what to do with it.

Over the years I've observed three common ways that parents get money into their child's hands:

- Allowance (either for doing chores or as a weekly stipend).
- Local Job (hourly wage).
- Entrepreneur (start a business).

The first one of these comes from sharing the family's money, as contrasted to the second and third which are earnings made outside the home. Let's start at home where they say all charity begins and cover the subject of allowance.

In-home Earning: Allowance

I was kidding when I wrote "charity" above, but only partially. In fact, that is the most controversial topic associated with allowance. Do kids have to complete chores to get paid or do they get the money because they are part of the family and need it to learn fiscal responsibility?

Rather than attempt to answer the question, let me give you two different points of view:

- *Money because you're part of the family:* Some experts would say that the advantage of this position is how well it dovetails with my opening argument that kids need money in their hands to be able to practice.
- *Money for chores:* Other experts would say (in a much softer way): "Get on the planet. In the real world you don't get something for nothing. Teach them now so they get that before the real world does it in a much rougher fashion." There is a lot of logic to this viewpoint as well. The disadvantage is that a child who gets paid for chores can blow off the chores if they don't want the money any particular week...and you can't really fire them for laying down on the job. This could also lead to an even longer-term problem—they stop making their bed in college because they're not getting paid any more to do it.
- *Middle ground:* There is also the philosophy of doing a combination of both. It's possible to give your child a smaller base allowance, that is not tied to basic chores (which they are expected to do as part of the family) and then give them a bonus for jobs that go above and beyond like raking the leaves or mowing the lawn.

You might want to get creative here as there is no one right answer to this question. Rather, do what works for you and is best for your family. Just promise me you'll do something instead of doing nothing.

The Allowance Contract

Kids often have selective memories. Meaning, you planned exactly what words you were going to use when describing how allowance is going to work in your home. But for some reason, three months later, they seem to have amnesia about the details of that conversation. Instead, they blurt out, "You never said that!" Maybe they're right; maybe you forgot to say that. I know there have been many times where I thought that I told my kids something, but it never left my head, made it to my mouth, and then traveled across the air to their ears.

Here's how we avoid that playing out in your house. Create a written contract where they go through and initial each part, and you both cosign the document. And where do you get such a contract? Google! There are plenty of samples of allowance contracts online. One of my favorites is from "Finance in the Classroom"[4] but feel free to choose from the many that are made available for free.

How Much to Give Them

I can be guaranteed that with every speech I give, this question comes up. They're your kids. Each child is different. They are all unique. However, here is the guiding tenet: Give them as much as you would have spent on them anyway—within reason. The goal is to teach them to use the money in the manner that you would have used it, only that they are *practicing* while you are still *paying* for it regardless.

Not good enough? You want an answer? Okay, here is a starting point. Give them a dollar for every year old they are. The six-year-old gets $6 and the nine-year-old gets $9. This math may not work later when a fifteen-year-old needs more than $15 a week. But by that time, they might be working outside the home.

What Age to Start Allowance

Once you have gained clarity on where you stand on this question, let's dig into some of the fine points, beginning with what the proper

---

4   https://financeintheclassroom.org/downloads/AllowanceContract.pdf

age is to start an allowance. This might surprise you, but I think you can start your kids off around 6 years old. Now, if your kid is 16 and has never received an allowance—it's okay. I promise we will get you up to speed.

In fact, you can actually start an allowance at any age. What is important is that allowance is set up well, and that the terms for receiving said allowance are fulfilled. To set up receiving an allowance, you're going to reach back into the parent archive stash of speeches you give to your kids over their lifetime. No, skip the "I'm So Disappointed in Your Behavior" (aka Speech #54). You're looking for Speech #88: "Allowance is a Privilege." Note: The script I am giving you is designed to start a younger age child off on the allowance path on the right foot, so you might need to modify it if you are talking to a 14-year-old. Or you can keep the childlike enthusiasm if you want to return the aggravation they are undoubtedly causing you!

Parent: "Congratulations <insert child's name>! Today is a big birthday for you. Do you know why?"

(Pause to let them give an answer knowing that they probably have zero idea of what's coming next.)

Parent: "Because at <insert age> you get the great responsibility and privilege of sharing some of the family's resources. What that means is that every Sunday you're going to get a little bit of money called an allowance. Do you know what an allowance is?"

(Keep going. They might have no clue what an allowance is and at this point you had them at the word "money," so they don't really care what you're about to say next. I suggest adding it regardless for those of you who have that unique kid that thinks at a higher level.)

Parent: "An allowance is money that is regularly (weekly) used by you to pay for things and help you practice with money. Every Sunday you are going to get $_____. When you get that money, you are going to divide it between three jars: Save, Spend, and Charity. Next week, I'll start to teach you what each of those jars are about when you have real money in your hands to decide where *our* money should go. How does that sound?"

There are lessons in this book on saving and on charity, but here you will want to explain the concept of the three jars (or, if your child is older, these may be related bank accounts).

- SAVING: This is the jar where they are going to put away money for something they need (we all know it's not a need… it's a want…but why ruin the fun).

  * Parent: "We know that there are going to be things that you want to buy. We also know that $6 might not be enough to pay for that item right now. You will put the money that you are holding to buy that item in the SAVE jar. This jar has a bonus. For every $1 that you put in, we (the parents) will put in another $1 for you. That way we are helping you toward your savings goal. If you like, you can put a picture of what you want on this jar as a reminder of what you are saving for."

  ✓ *Side Note:* This may seem like you are bribing them. I admit that's what I'm telling you to do. But don't be mad at yourself; your intentions are good—to give them a little nudge in using that jar. Remember, Americans are notoriously bad at saving—but that's because they didn't have a parent like you who is willing to bribe.

- SPENDING: This is similar to your checking account. Money is meant to go in this jar and then right out again. This is for normal, run-of-the-mill expenses that your son/daughter will have. It might be a candy bar, an ice cream cone, or going to the movies. It's not a goal that they are saving for.

  ✳ <u>Parent:</u> "You have some things that you like to have every week. For example, during the baseball season you like to buy baseball cards. From now on this is your expense, not ours. Since you need a place to keep that money until we get to go to the store, you can put it in the spend jar."

  ✓ *Side Note:* No bribing here. It's not that you don't want them to spend, in fact, you're kind of forcing the issue by making them pay for things. But this jar gets no incentive. It's just like in life when you get an incentive for putting money in your company's retirement plan, but don't get an incentive for money that is paying for your food and mortgage.

- CHARITY: This one is easy and your best opportunity to help create a community-centric and not an ego-centric child. Here is where you are going to try and teach them about giving to others. That's not easy, even for us adults. But let's give it a try.

  ✳ <u>Parent:</u> "It's important to our family that we try to help others. Don't you think that's important? Sometimes we accomplish that by doing things for others—physically going somewhere like when we went to the soup kitchen to help give out meals. Do you remember that? At other times, we are going to thoughtfully give money. But we must have saved that money somewhere so it's available when we are ready or asked to give. It's so important to us that every week we set aside money for this jar. So at least $1 every week goes in this jar. The good news is that for every $1 you put in, we (the parents) will put in another $2 as a match. That's how important we think it is, and that's why it gets the biggest match."

OUTSIDE-THE-HOME EARNINGS: LOCAL JOBS AND ENTREPRENEURSHIP

For your older child, earning money outside of the home can be the perfect opportunity to encourage them to use a few hours of their week productively to make some money. There is plenty of time, and instead of getting frustrated as you watch them wasting those valuable hours in front of a screen, inspire them to get a job. A decent job will also help them "avoid trouble" that sometimes comes when kids have too much time on their hands.

A job also teaches a young adult basic levels of responsibility in terms of having to be somewhere on time, and make choices between that obligation and other things that might seem more appealing (like going to the beach). They also need to listen to a different set of authority figures, their bosses. And it gives you, the parent, another opportunity to cope with the fact that they seem to listen to everyone else more than you!

There are other great money lessons that come from your child having a job. Working:

- exposes them to adult financial concepts;
- builds their financial self-esteem;
- helps them understand the value of a dollar;
- develops gratitude for the hours you (the parent) work to pay the bills;
- introduces them to paying taxes in a way that is relevant to them;
- gives them practice marketing themselves for job opportunities; and

- introduces them to the concept of supply and demand.

In addition to those financial literacy benefits, they also start to build their own work resume (including potential references for other jobs in the future). All in all, this makes a job one of the best life lessons they could experience at a time where their studies are not in competition with their potential work hours.

Local Job (Hourly Wage) vs. Entrepreneurship
Probably the most common method for your young adult child to earn money is to get a local job. These come in all shapes and sizes but typically involve earning an hourly wage. (In some states there are also legal rules around the age at which children can get a job, so be sure to check them.) Examples of jobs for young teenagers that I've seen from the town I live in include:

- landscaping during the summer months;
- busboy/girl at the local restaurants/diners; and
- scooping ice cream at the local ice cream shop.

Many of you might have had babysitting come to mind, but I would put that in a different category—being an entrepreneur. Both types of jobs are helpful, although your child might naturally fall into one category more than another based on their personality and interests.

Some of your kids will have that entrepreneurial mindset. This starts with the lemonade stand and then moves into more sophisticated business ideas such as:

- babysitting;
- tutoring;

- individual sports training (where a high school kid gives one-on-one lessons to a younger child);
- lawn mowing, snow shoveling, etc.;
- making and selling a craft; or
- creating the next great Facebook or app (this one could also help your retirement).

This avenue takes a bit more thought, creativity, and planning. If you are going to venture down the "start your own business" path, you will want to start with a brainstorm. There is no such thing as a dumb idea during the brainstorming process. Good ideas can come from a lot of sources: problems needing solutions, innovative ideas to create products/services, or even things that benefit a charity or greater purpose. Be sure to use a mind map to optimize this process by giving it structure. A digital mind map (which can be found at www.mindmeister.com) is a fun and efficient way to get your ideas on "paper" and basically storyboard them so they are properly thought out. You can then collaborate with others by emailing/texting it to them to get their input.

You also might want to take advantage of asking someone to be a mentor for your entrepreneurial child; someone who has been down that road. I've reminded my own children, *ad nauseam,* of the old saying: "Experience is a great teacher." The life lessons of being entrepreneurial are the same as the ones I mentioned above but also include gross versus net revenues (that basically means how much money they're pulling in compared to what they are really making), and marketing (how are we getting people to buy from them).

As your child grows up, and starts earning some real money, you will need to decide where it goes once it's earned. Perhaps the piggy banks labeled SAVE, SPEND, and CHARITY have become linked bank accounts with a debit card, while retaining the principle of dividing the money before it all goes away in a whirlwind spend-a-thon.

At the end of the day, it's vitally important that you get money into the hands of your child so they can practice. How you do that is a personal choice. Just promise me you'll do it in some way, shape, or form.

For more information on this lesson, scan the QR code to visit our website.

Lesson Two: Teach Them the Value of a Dollar

Kids understand the value of a dollar just fine.
That's why they'd rather use your dollar than theirs.

A COMMON COMPLAINT OF MOST parents while their kids are young is: "My kid doesn't know the value of a dollar." As we will see, that isn't always or exactly true. But to the degree that it is, it is probably because they haven't been taught the value of a dollar! If most of their expenses are paid for by you, the parent, how would they know? Think about how you got an appreciation for what a dollar is truly worth. Growing up, you gradually had to pay for bigger and bigger items and hopefully earned more and more money to accompany and account for those expenses.

It is the same with our children. The items that your child typically pays for himself/herself are usually the lower cost items such as a movie ticket or a meal at their favorite fast-food place. They may understand the difference between a shirt that costs $20 and a shirt that costs $100, and how relatively easy it might be to talk a parent into the former expenditure, while the latter one may require contributing some money saved through earnings or gift money. (They may also have mastered the art of knowing which parent to ask for what, but we'll leave that discussion for the time being!)

In our kids' minds, however, there is no real bridge between those lower cost items and the costs of a car, a home, or college. It's one thing for them to understand that a slice of pizza costs $3. It's something else completely for them to understand that their college education will cost over $300,000.

Our kids are just like us. If they are making their own money, say, babysitting for $15 per hour, they can certainly appreciate the value of a $30 entree at a nice restaurant. In their minds, they now have a reference point: "This meal would have cost me 2 hours of babysitting at the neighbor's house." But that still doesn't mean they can appreciate it when you write a $30,000 tuition check for their schooling—they can't, because they have no frame of reference from which to do so. They can do the math on their cellphone calculator that shows them they would have to babysit Cindy, 24 hours a day, for three months to make that much at $15/hr. I'm joking, of course, but the point is serious: this is why their reactions seem insensitive and entitled—not because they are bad people.

The complaint that a child doesn't understand the value of a dollar is typically used at a time when the parent has laid out money for something for the child and felt disrespected because they didn't get the proper amount of gratitude in response. How do we encourage the proper gratitude for you shelling out your hard-earned cash, and perhaps more important, instill this concept before your child gets into the world of having to budget for themselves?

I have a solution to present to you, but first let me say I understand the reticence most parents feel about telling their kids how much money they earn. Many parents are appalled the first time their child asks, "How much do you make?" Our kids don't know—until we tell them—that this particular question is off limits in just about every social circle. It also wouldn't really help matters much, as even a reasonable amount of earnings will result in a number that is too large for them to effectively comprehend. If Mom earns $100K a year, what does that mean? 33,000 slices of pizza?

However, there is an opportunity to redirect the question into one which helps them figure out the value of a dollar and how much you must be earning collectively, even roughly, to sustain the family's lifestyle—without your having to tell them the actual income number. And that is a deep dive into the family's budget.

HOW MUCH DOES IT COST TO RAISE YOU?

If you've ever gone through a budgeting exercise to figure out your household expenses, you will quickly learn that a good percentage of your expenses are attributable to costs related to your kids. It only takes a stroll through your checkbook, credit card statement, ATM withdrawals, and Venmo transactions to start to add up the costs of raising a child. And if you haven't created a household budget already—it is time. It is part of the financial planning process, and if you are serious about teaching your child about money, then there are certain steps you will need to take yourself; this is a recurring theme in our process.

Some families have a spreadsheet that they've created which outlines what it costs to run their household. This list includes everything: groceries, mortgage, car payments, vacations—you name it. If you have created a household budget, it's time to break it out and share with the kids, but not before you've asked them to do some thinking first.

You can start by asking them to brainstorm a list of all the "things" the family spends money on for them personally. As they rack their brains, you can assist them with some of the major areas in which a family usually has expenses:

- Clothes.
- Food.

- School (tuition, supplies, other).
- Sports.
- Lessons.
- Tutoring.
- House (their portion).
- Transportation (include some of the car payment, gas, insurance).
- Vacations.

It might be helpful to hang the list on your refrigerator or somewhere that is visible to your entire family. Once you have a solid list in hand, you can add the monthly or annual dollar expenditures which you'll use later to track the final amount. If you find yourself uneasy or even embarrassed about how much money you are spending in a certain area (dining out, hobby expenditures) that can be taken as a sign that you might want to change your own spending habits. Keeping this information from your children won't make the effects of your own choices go away.

GO BIG PICTURE

At this point, you might bring in the following statistics from The U.S. Department of Agriculture. This government agency puts out data which talks about the cost of raising a child today. In their last study, they claimed that the average cost in the U.S. was $230,000. Now we all know that the amount can vary dramatically depending on the area of the country in which one lives. For example, that same source said that in the urban northeast the amount was more like $264,000. If you live in a fairly affluent area, those costs might go well above $300,000. And that doesn't even include college.

How does your household budget for the year stack up against these numbers? If you were to take the yearly amount and multiply it by 18 (although we know that the expenses don't stop when a kid goes to college!) are you in the ballpark? Are you and your child forgetting important items?

Another interesting statistic to reflect on is how different categories of spending break down in the typical American household. Spending in various areas might look something like this:

1. Housing (29%)
2. Food (18%)
3. Education (16%)
4. Transportation (15%)
5. Health care (9%)
6. Clothing (6%)
7. Miscellaneous other expenses (7%)[5]

Of course, these percentages could vary widely. These numbers should not be gospel in your dialogue with children, but rather conversation starters. In fact, I think it would be fun to lay out the above-mentioned categories to your kids without the percentages and help them chop up what they feel might be the allocation in your own household. After you've had everyone "place their bets," you can then move into the actual calculations within your own house based on the budget you have been putting together.

As your budget gets more specific, you may find some of the discomfort of revealing how much money you and/or your spouse earn creep back in other ways. For example, should your child know how much it costs to own or rent your home? Should they know how much your car costs, and whether it was purchased new or leased? My opinion is that they do need to know these things. To soften the blow or introduce

---

[5]   https://www.usda.gov/media/blog/2017/01/13/cost-raising-child

greater context, you can talk about homes that were bought and sold in your town (easily gotten information from online public records), or chat about new cars that are coming out and how much they cost.

THAT $250,000 LIFETIME COST

Converting the yearly household budget into the lifetime cost of having a child can be a fun connection to make once you have it completely filled out. Have your child go through the household budget and isolate the things the family spends money on primarily because of them. Some of these items will be easy, others they will have to think about. For example, if there are four people living in the home, then every family dinner has 25% of the cost attributed to it to that individual child. (Or perhaps 15%–20% if they are ordering less expensive meals and hopefully not having any alcohol with dinner!)

This can lead to discussions which further illuminate the value of a dollar, such as:

- *Are older kids more or less expensive?* While bringing a child into the world is not a cheap endeavor—illustrated by the costs of baby gear and diapers—nothing compares to the costs of children as they get older. Add in a new driver into your household (with the cost of the car, gas, and insurance . . . oh, that darn insurance) and you can really watch your costs escalate. If you have a larger gap in ages between your kids, you might have them "face off" in a challenge to see who is less of an economic burden to the household. Your teenager might be able to peg the cost of childcare on a younger sibling, for example. In any event, it is a spirited debate which will be a stealth way of cementing the concept in their heads.

- *Is there a discount to having more than one child?* In the USDA's study they claimed that families with 3 or more children spend an average of 24% less per child. Remember, that isn't 24% less on a total cost of one child. If it was $250,000 per child, and you have 3 children, while it doesn't cost $750,000 it still costs $570,000. I wanted to remind you of that before you started to root for triplets on the next birthing in your home. The USDA says that's because children often share bedrooms in bigger families, clothing and toys are handed down, and food can be purchased in larger and more economical packages. Also, private schools and childcare providers may offer sibling discounts.

- *Are things more expensive now, or less, and how?* One added cost that today's generation of parents has that maybe wasn't a line-item in our parents' era is childcare. Another cost may be extracurricular sports. Back in our day, our coaches were typically the mom or dad of a player on the team. Today's child is more likely to grow up with nonparent paid coaches for their sports teams starting from as young as 6 years old.

Now don't think that these conversations are automatically going to lead to your child having gratitude for all the money you're doling out for them. There is a chance, however, that your son/daughter will look at things a little differently and at least understand that growing up is not free. It also plants the seed that one day, they get the unbelievable honor of getting to pick up all those expenses on their own.

For more information on this lesson, scan the QR code to visit our website.

LESSON THREE:
SHOW THEM HOW TO BUDGET

If balance is a key to life—then so is budgeting.

As we saw in the previous lesson about helping your child understand the value of a dollar, introducing your kids to the household budget—however uncomfortable that might be—is a crucial step in helping them to understand what money is and what money does. It is a natural next step, then, for them to go from the larger household budget to establishing their own microbudgets. But even though budgeting is key to financial success, it is a topic that is avoided, even at the adult level.

Behavioral finance experts have a field day talking about why American households procrastinate creating a budget. But it's pretty straightforward. People don't want to talk about it because if they do, they may have to make changes to their spending habits.

However, if you can find a way to implant the concept of budgeting into your kids' brains, they will grow up with a healthy attitude on the subject, won't avoid it, and as such will have a much better chance of achieving a secure financial future—maybe better than our generation.

Budgeting can be defined simply as: *deciding what our priorities are and structuring our financial situation accordingly.* Done right, this allocation of resources gives one the ability to spend without guilt, assuming they've included adequate saving as part of their budget.

The truth of the matter is that if you, the parent, don't have your own budgeting in order then it's embarrassing trying to teach your own kids. But DON'T STOP READING HERE BECAUSE YOU'RE AFRAID. This is the time where you need to finally get sick and tired of being sick and tired. You can muster some courage and, even if you are making mistakes, be transparent and tell them where you need to improve. Make it a family project that you can work on together, hold each other accountable, and do it as a team. They can learn from both your mistakes and victories. You need to have the confidence to admit that you are human and not mistake-free. If you need more on this one, read Brene Brown's book, *The Gifts of Imperfection.*

Let's go through the four steps to have a fruitful family conversation on the topic of budgeting.

STEP 1: DEFINE WHAT A BUDGET IS

Having a budget means making sure the amount you spend aligns with how much you earn. Since your kids have been through the household budgeting exercise previously, you can now go into how this affects them. Having them make a budget that is personalized lets them think through all the expenses that are attributable to only them and go through their own process. It might even be easier with a lot less money coming in and out to see how the concept of financial trade-offs can become even more crystallized.

STEP 2: BRAINSTORM THE CATEGORIES OF OUTFLOWS

This one is best done with old fashioned pen and paper. Have them brainstorm a list of all their personal outflows. You don't have to overload them with one of those nice budgeting lists you may have found on the internet. Let them struggle through the list over a few days and try to add to the initial brainstormed list over the course of a week. Give them the joy of adding to the list as if they found something in a scavenger hunt. You will find that this might be a bit of a reality check for them.

STEP 3: FINALIZE THE CATEGORY LIST

Here is where you can help them think of all the categories that might apply to them. They probably know about their entertainment, specifically, food; and you have already introduced the concept of saving and donating in addition to simply spending. But how far down the road can they look? What about next year's fashions or the technology that might be available in two years? Is there a tux that will need to be rented for a prom in three years? This isn't to say that you as a parent are going to expect them to pay for all of this based on what they earn, simply that you want them to get familiar with everything that is spent on them or that they spend. Of course, all of these ideas are enhanced when the children are either earning allowance or their own money from a job outside of the house. As we saw in the first lesson, getting money into their hands is crucial so they can begin to practice how budgeting works in the real world—that's their world if you haven't figured that out yet.

STEP 4: TWEAK AND FORMALIZE THE REVISED BUDGET

This is typically when you begin a conversation about Needs vs. Wants, otherwise known as the distinction between fixed versus discretionary expenses.

It is here where you can ask your kids questions such as: *Do you see any adjustments we should be considering to your current budget? Are there any areas where you feel you are overspending, in proportion to how much enjoyment you are getting? If you had more money, what would be the areas that you would want to increase first? (Never a bad idea to plant the seed that more money is a good thing!)*

At the end of this stage, you can print out your child's revised budget and then bring it out on a quarterly basis for dinnertime conversation. Hint: Put that as a recurring reminder in your calendar so it literally pops up on your calendar for you to bring up the conversation at dinner that quarter. Doing so will keep it front of mind for both you and them. These periodic reminders will set them on the road of budgeting themselves as soon as they get their first job out of college. Ultimately that helps you, as parents, eventually remove them as one of your budget items.

 For more information on this lesson, scan the QR code to visit our website.

LESSON FOUR: ENCOURAGE THEM TO SAVE

Save first. Then spend. Never in the reverse order.

TEACHING YOUR KIDS HOW TO save is one of the crucial skills for you as a parent to impart, and why we began this process with its very own jar from their first allowance (if you started them in elementary school). As a financial advisor, I've had a front-row seat with my adult clients to see what habits are crucial for grown-ups to achieve financial success. Most people mistakenly think that choosing the right investments is what creates financial security. But if you don't have the right amount of capital available to be invested, some incredibly great rate of return—which likely will not hold up in the long-term—is not a realistic way to solve the problem of one's lack of savings. What gets you to financial security is your ability to save regularly over time. My experience tells me this is a learned ability; it is not innate. All the more reason to start educating your children on this subject of good financial habits as soon as they are able to comprehend it.

Which, it turns out, is pretty early. The subject matter of saving dovetails nicely with that of "delayed gratification." You have almost certainly heard about the Stanford marshmallow experiment. This was a research experiment conducted in 1972 where a child was offered a choice between a small but immediate reward, such as a marshmallow, which they could eat right away, or two marshmallows if they waited for about 15 minutes. What researchers found was that the children who were able to wait had higher SAT scores, healthier physiques and, generally, better life outcomes. Pretty impressive for waiting fifteen minutes, right?

SAMANTHA SAVER AND PAUL PROCRASTINATOR

The kids who were able to wait were in essence saving their one marshmallow. It's almost as if that marshmallow grew over time by the miracle of compound interest, a concept which we will discuss on the next page. You can try this experiment with your younger child. If they choose the immediate gratification, don't worry that their entire life will end up a shambles—talk them through the benefits of the waiting.

In Lesson One, I introduced the concept of the three jars: SAVE/SPEND/CHARITY. For younger kids to learn how to save, I do recommend physical objects, such as jars, for them to put their money into while older kids can have separate but linked bank accounts. But I don't recommend the typical, nicely painted ceramic piggy bank. Why? Because you can't see the money once it's in the piggy bank! If you have to use a piggy bank, at least use one that is clear. You want the money to be visible. And with coins, you can see them stack up, even though your child might not understand the difference between a penny, a nickel, a dime, or a quarter. It's important that the younger kids see the amount of money piling up and getting closer to the top of the clear bank. Even better, see if you can find a clear piggy bank that has three chambers which you can label SAVE/SPEND/CHARITY. That sends the message that every dollar has its place.

For the older kids who are growing out of their childhood (i.e., want to be cool), you can begin to engage them with some hard numbers to back up the value of saving. They may not yet have seen the common example of two people who are saving for retirement that demonstrates the power of starting early. Vanguard has some great data on their website which shows this comparison:

Samantha Saver started saving at age 25 and put away $10,000 per year. And then, at age 40, she stopped saving. Paul Procrastinator, on the other hand, was a little behind; he didn't get started until age 35. He also invested $10,000 per year but he did so for the next 30 years (until age 65). If both accounts earned a 6% annual rate of return, it seems like Paul would end up with more money, because he contributed more over time, right? Yet, take a look at who had more money at the end:

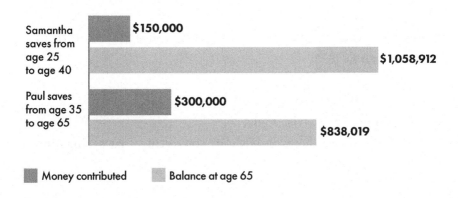

This example of compound interest (see the next lesson for more) clearly makes the case for starting to save as soon as possible. Compounding works best when you get the money into your account early to have it start working for you. This is what allowed Samantha Saver to invest half the money and still come out with significantly more than Paul Procrastinator.

BUILDING THE HABIT

Saving is a habit. And like all good habits, it takes some work to create. Depending on the age of your child, you can start by setting some short-term savings goals. You might encourage them to use the allowance they are getting to start saving for something they want, or if they are already working, you can have them take a percentage of their income and put it away—but not for some unknown purpose in the distant future, but rather for something that they want right now (or soon).

Regardless of your child's age, here is the key. Do you remember in the "Getting Money into Their Hands" section when I suggested bribing a child by putting $1 away in their savings for every $1 they place there? Well, you can even match at a higher rate—one that is unheard of, making you the most generous employer in the history of employers. It can be like matching $3 for every $1 they put in (Or $20 for every $10, if they are older). You'll have plenty of time to slowly lower that or change the terms, but to get them going, you simply want them to experience three things:

1. Actually save something
2. Get to their savings goal
3. Appreciate the experience of converting that savings into a purchase

Make sure you understand that saving, as a skill, is 90% about habits. Those skills are best developed when your child is young and reinforced as they mature until they get their first job out of college.

PAY YOURSELF FIRST

Learning how to save is the same as paying yourself first. That is a phrase you can drill into your child's head, over and over—until they beg you to stop. But don't stop, simply because it is one of the oldest wealth building principles in history.

Here is a visual you can share with your child:

Which is You?

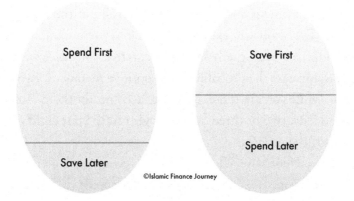

Spend First

Save First

Save Later

Spend Later

©Islamic Finance Journey

The "save first then spend" mantra is mission critical toward successfully building a secure nest egg. The more you drive this home, the greater the likelihood they'll make sure to enroll in that 401(k) the minute it is offered at their first job and end up as Samantha Saver.

In these diagrams, it seems like the amount of savings on the left, after spending, might be approximately 20%, whereas the saving first on the right side is more like 60%. The reason is that we inevitably save more when we do it first, treating it as a bill, rather than just save what is left over at the end of a month which is always less.

For the sake of your kids, you might want to start with a savings goal of 10%. It is an arbitrary amount, but at least it will serve as a conversation starter. We are trying to build habits and use the least amount of math possible to encourage their making it a regular process.

For younger kids you can position the conversation as follows (after telling them the importance of saving): "For every dollar we earn, it's a good habit to put 10 cents away in savings."

As your child gets a bit older, you can memorialize the process by visiting a local bank or credit union to give them a picture in their head as to where the money goes that they are seeing in their online account. I would suggest that you touch base with the bank ahead of time to set up an appointment and make sure they roll out the red carpet for your child. You want the experience to be as memorable as possible. That includes ensuring the bank representative you meet with is "kid friendly" to increase the probability of a positive memory for your child. Of course, while you are there, set up an account for them. Then make sure you go back two or three times per year until your child gets comfortable with the process.

If you'd prefer to use 5% or 20% for a savings goal, go for it. I don't think the percentage is as important as just developing the habit of saving. I've found that with certain clients, I need to start small so they don't worry that their lifestyle will be affected too dramatically. When they see that it hasn't been by a 5% savings habit, the next year I can always have them move it up to 7%, then 9%, then 15%, then 20% and they won't even feel it. Slow and steady wins the race.

Stress to your children the importance of saving a portion of every dollar they earn. Otherwise, they may never reach financial security. If you don't start saving money, there is no magical money fairy that is going to save it for you. Whether it be from allowance, a job, or even a gift, always save a portion of it.

As a parent, you will know whether you've succeeded or failed to communicate the value of saving when you eventually ask your now young adult this question: "When you signed up for your new benefits plan, did you enroll in your 401(k)?"

If they did, mission accomplished! If they didn't, prepare the guest room for them for later in life.

For more information on this lesson, scan the QR code to visit our website.

Lesson Five: Educate Them on Compound Interest

*Earning interest on your interest—
that's the key to wealth building.*

It was Albert Einstein who made compound interest famous when he said:

> *"Compound interest is the eighth wonder of the world. He who understands it, earns it … he who doesn't … pays it."*

Far be it for us to argue with Einstein. As I stressed in the previous lesson, we need to do a decent job telling our kids that they should save. In this lesson, we need to tell them what will happen ideally with that savings. It will grow … while we are off making money to add to that savings pot.

I like to explain it this way: Interest is like a rental fee. Banks are using your money to loan out to their patrons and then charge those customers more for its use than they are paying you. Kids may wonder where the extra money goes, and we can point to the beautiful buildings that house many banks … but also acknowledge that sometimes people default on their loans and discuss the concept of having good credit. You may even want to broach the subject of a credit "score" with them briefly (see Lesson Eight for more information), and then return to the main topic of this chapter: interest itself.

The goal is to give our kids a firm understanding of what compound interest is, and why it is important—namely because inflation ends up ravaging anyone's purchasing power. One dollar put away now where it can generate no interest, such as stashed in a mattress, is not one dollar in the future when they may need to use it. In fact, it might only be a mere fraction of it. By not earning interest, a person is actually spending money with nothing to show for it—otherwise known as losing money.

Inflation of a Dollar

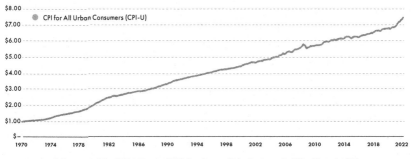

Source U.S. Bureau of Labor Statistics, CPI for All Urban Consumers (CPI-U), Chart shows monthly data from January 1st, 1970 to February 1st, 2022

A person who understands compound interest, on the other hand, is further motivated to develop the habit of saving—which is exactly where you want your child to be. But this begins, of course, with helping children understand what interest is, which is why it makes sense to start with simple interest. From there we'll move onto compound interest.

Simple Interest

I would initially steer clear of giving your kids a complex formula involving principal x interest rate x time or anything like that. Let's start simply, with simple interest—as the name indicates!

Imagine you gave the bank $100. If they were paying you 10% simple interest, what would they give you after the first year? We use 10% (even though as a rate it is too high to be realistic) because it's easier math to start with.

Now, draw a picture like this:

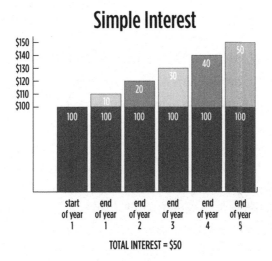

Simple Interest

TOTAL INTEREST = $50

Compound Interest

Here's where things start to get fun. We explain that the money they put into a savings account earns interest. Since it's their money they not only get to keep the interest, but also it gets added to their account. And now because it is part of their total pot of money, they can *earn interest on the interest!*

Let's play the same game we did earlier with simple interest but now in a 10% compounding interest world.

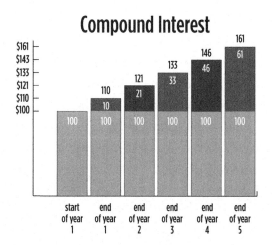

Compound Interest

They can see that simple interest produced $50 and compound interest earned them $61. Aren't you glad that you listened to me and used 10% as your interest rate now? Much easier math, right?

RULE OF 72

One of the best party tricks you can teach your kids is the Rule of 72. Basically, this method is used to estimate how long it takes your money to double. It reinforces the compound interest concept. Here is the rule:

If you take 72 and divide it by the interest rate you intend to get, the result will be the number of years it takes to double your money. Sticking with 10%, if you divide 72 by 10, you will find that it takes you 7.2 years to double your money.

Now start playing this game and make your kids figure it out using different rates of return (interest rates):

1% = 72 years
2% = 36 years
3% = 24 years

4% = 18 years
5% = 14.4 years
6% = 12 years
7% = 10.3 years

You can have math contests with the kids on the couch, in the car, while taking a walk, or spot check your child by stopping them in the hallway and blurt at them:

Parent: "QUICK. Rule of 72. How many years does it take for your money to double at 4%? Quick, quick, quick."

The first couple of times they'll hesitate and get stuck. But soon they'll know it's coming, and they will be ready for you. Great—this is a game you want them to win! If you find both kids sitting in the living room at the same time, have them square off against each other with the first person to get it wins the quick draw.

ONLINE CALCULATORS AND FUN GAMES

Now you can let the kids return to their comfort zone and use an online calculator. Visit my website for some of my favorites. Hopefully, the one you choose will have graphs of an exponential curve so they can see the mountain chart of that compounding interest. One of my favorites is MSN Money because it has a number of different factors that they can tinker with based on their curiosity.

There are also fun games you can find online. My favorite is from Money Prodigy: they call it Compound Interest Ager. Basically, you go on http://www.in20years.co/ to get a doctored picture of your child at an older age and then have them run a compound interest calculator on how much they'll have when they reach that age (using the hypothetical examples on the calculator I shared with you). I found it pretty funny when I've done it with my own kids. And on the serious side, it reinforces to kids—whose idea of the future may be tenuous at best—that they will, in fact, age. Now will their money grow alongside them?

My second favorite game was put out by Policygenius Inc., an unaffiliated insurance broker, which suggested an outdoor activity. The part of this game that appealed to me was that they made it into an athletic event. The basic gist is to set up a small basket on the driveway at a height where the kids can reach in, but can't see in. Then choose a spot at the opposite end of the driveway as a landmark. Each child is given a roll of quarters and told to put a quarter in the basket. Then they are instructed to walk/run to the landmark and back; one round trip simulates a month. Each time they reach the basket, they throw in another quarter. This continues until all 40 quarters are in the basket.

While the kids are in earshot, Dad/Mom puts varying combinations of pennies, nickels, and dimes into the basket after each quarter goes in. That sound of their parents' money creates a little curiosity. When the 40th quarter goes in, you let them see what's inside the basket, and that simulates interest being paid on their money. Then use that money to go out and buy ice cream. You can use candy instead of coins and have the same lesson. Just don't eat it all at once.

The bottom line is this: The idea of money growing is much more intriguing than the thought of money alone. Try these ideas on for size and watch your kids' *interest compound!*

For more information on this lesson, scan the QR code to visit our website.

LESSON SIX: EXPOSE THEM TO INVESTING

Never make a killing, never get killed.

W E'VE COVERED A LOT OF TOPICS ahead of investing. Getting money in your kids' hands, how to save, what budgeting is ... these are just a few examples of areas you'll want to make sure your child has a grasp on before you venture down the road of creating the next Warren Buffett. But investing is a crucial topic to discuss with your kids. The question is, how?

When the topic of investing comes up, parents oftentimes get excited and want to jump right into teaching kids to buy individual stocks. In my opinion, that is not the place to start. If we are trying to instill financial literacy in our children, we have to get them to walk before they can run. Teaching kids to "pick a winner" before they have a basic foundation of core financial principles is like trying to teach a youth basketball player to dunk before you teach them how to dribble the ball. Dunking is cool ... but there is no dunking until they can dribble the ball to the basket to make that dunk.

Think about it. Will most young adults be able to grow their investment skillset and have the time/energy to apply these skills properly—in addition to their day job? The answer is likely no. To do that would mean they would have to get their financial investment acumen to a high enough level to manage their own portfolio, across all the asset classes (and geographic regions), and maintain a diversified portfolio. It is highly unlikely they would be able to take this effort on and perform well as a newly-minted adult. I've been a financial advisor for 27 years and I don't even buy individual company stocks for myself. I think that says a lot.

In brief, learning about individual stocks is the sizzle, but I'd implore you to stick with the steak. Let's think about this conversation in terms of "buckets." Yes, buckets where investors put their money based on different goals and objectives. And that is teaching your child how to invest with the following four steps:

STEP 1: KNOW YOUR TIME HORIZON

Helping your child to understand their time horizon might be the biggest factor in determining how they are going to ultimately invest their money. We can think about the "bucket conversation" by simply dividing one's money up into three buckets:

- $ Now – This is money that your child plans on using in the very near future. This is their spending money for going to the movies, eating out, or buying gifts for friends. Obviously, this is money that they need to keep safe and liquid.
- $ Later – Here is where you put money that isn't needed right now, but you do have plans for in the not-so-far future. For an adult, this might mean that you need it in the next five years. For kids, it's more like three years.
- $ Much Later – "Much later" means different things to different people. For adults we usually associate this with retirement savings. For kids, retirement savings is a great concept but the furthest their minds might be able to envision as for "much later" is buying a home.

Here are two different examples of scenarios to help your child determine how much risk they should take in their investment portfolio based on their time horizon:

1. They have $18,000 they need to use for college next year, which would naturally lead to taking lower risks.
2. They received $1,000 in gift money in 7th grade and plan on using this money to buy their first car in 12th grade, which is enough of a time horizon that they may want to be a little more aggressive with their choice of investments.

The closer your child gets to the time that money is going to be needed, the less time you'll have for your portfolio to recoup a sudden loss should the stock market suffer a significant drop (such as what occurred in 1987, 2000–02, 2008, and 2020 … to name a few). In short, make sure they know how long it will be until they realistically need to use this money—that will guide the next step.

STEP 2: UNDERSTAND RISK VERSUS REWARD

As I alluded to in Step 1, the amount of time one's money is going to spend in each bucket is an important concept to understand before you move on to the risk/reward conversation. There is a saying we have in the investment advisory world that goes, "Time in the market, not timing the market." Basically this implies that the longer one keeps their money invested, the greater chance that historical investment performance reverts to the mean and allows you to ride out any short-term blips (that's a nice way to say "severe downturns" in the stock market). For this discussion, let's assume you assigned these time horizons to your different buckets:
- $ Now – Next week.
- $ Later – 3 years.

- $ Much Later – 8 years.

By now, many parents have learned the phrase: *Low risk, low return; high risk, high return.*

Nonetheless, it's hard for a young adult to really understand what that means. They get the general concept, but they have no clue which investment vehicles help you manage that risk. This is typically a good time to give them a top-down understanding of the many investment categories that one will use, in a diversified fashion, to meet their future savings goals. My favorite visual for teaching risk versus reward of investment products is this pyramid:

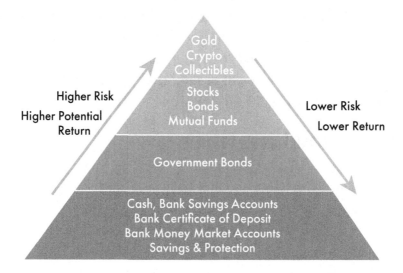

This image shows the risks/rewards of different types of investments. You can see that investments with lower risks and lower returns are at the bottom. This is what we would refer to as "stable asset classes." Investments that would fall into this foundational level of the investment pyramid include: cash, certificates of deposit, and money market accounts.

At the top of the chart, you see stocks, and while stocks historically give us healthy returns over the long run, that comes with a tremendous amount of volatility and risk during the short run.

STEP 3: ESTABLISH YOUR DIVERSIFICATION

Asset allocation was a topic that went largely unexplored until 1986, when Gary P. Brinson, CFA, Randolph Hood, and Gilbert L. Beebower (known collectively as BHB), asserted it was the single biggest determinant of investor returns—more than which securities are selected or market timing. Asset allocation is otherwise known as diversification.

Let's fill those buckets.
- $ Now – You'll want to have very safe and liquid investments.
- $ Later – Here you want to get a little higher rate of return than the money in your bank account, but you shouldn't swing for the fences.
- $ Much Later – This is the place where you can be aggressive and risk some "short-term pain toward long-term gains."

Try this chart on for size:

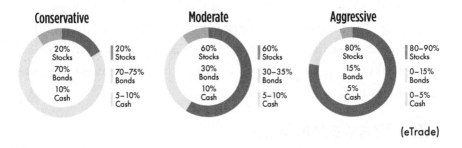

(eTrade)

What the chart implies is that for every level of risk, there is a corresponding asset allocation of diversifying assets that would align with risk tolerance. It is definitely an art, and not a science. As you have heard legal disclaimers say, "Past performance is not an indication of future results." That is definitely true, but it is still what the financial planning and asset management community uses to base their portfolio's diversification. Choosing a mix of stocks, bonds, alternative asset classes, and cash are the major categories one uses to help construct these portfolios. The longer time horizon you have to ride out the ups and downs of the market's volatility, the more comfortably you can move to the right on the risk scale provided this very important point:

Your child should only take on a risk level to the extent that they won't get overly emotional when the market goes down (and it will) causing them to want to take action and abandon their plan. Diversification only works if they stay the course in both up AND down markets.

In short, I would urge you not to teach your kids about individual stocks. Instead, spend the time teaching them about asset allocation. This is in part because trying to predict returns for various investments is a losing strategy. You can lump into that futility trying to guess how asset classes will perform relative to one another in the short run.

With all the choices out there in the financial marketplace today, picking out which stocks, bonds, mutual funds, ETFs, or money managers will be used to execute each part of a well-diversified portfolio is not easy to do. My preference is to stick with index funds or ETFs, as they give broader diversification than just one individual stock, they are low in fees, and they serve as a great starter kit for kids to understand how to fill in their "buckets of diversification."

STEP 4: MAINTAIN YOUR COURSE

This is not an exercise of setting a portfolio and then forgetting about it. There is a balance between looking at your portfolio too much versus not enough. Just because you set an asset allocation doesn't mean you never tweak it. It's important to monitor things from time to time and rebalance every so often. For kids, I think you just make this point and then rebalance twice per year.

By doing this, your kids make it a habit, and later, when they are no longer in your home and are in their adult lives, they can determine the frequency of the monitoring and rebalancing. By the time they get there, computers will likely have taken over this entire process and will do the monitoring and rebalancing for them.

There is a great chart for you to use, called the *Periodic Table of Investment Returns,* to talk about what's happened historically in the markets. Located in the Resources section of the Total Cents website, it reveals the importance of maintaining the course, and to get them thinking about rebalancing based on what's happened within the last year in certain asset classes.

If All of That Seemed Like a Lot …

At the end of the day you, as a parent, are looking for the little coachable moments. Those are opportunities that just pop up, in the flow of ordinary life, that enable you to teach investing to your child in a way that is natural to what's going on around them. That could mean showing them an account statement when it arrives in the mail and teaching them about asset allocation. Or it could be asking at the dinner table: "Did you happen to see what happened in the stock market today?" And when the iron is hot, and they show some interest, try to do a deeper dive on the information in this lesson. What happens if they don't show an interest? Find a way to broach the topic regardless. Although they might not appreciate it now, they certainly will later!

For more information on this lesson, scan the QR code to visit our website.

Lesson Seven: Break the News About Taxes

Taxes are what you get to pay for making money. The bad news is you're paying taxes. The good news is ... you're paying taxes.

I HAD TO LAUGH WHEN I HEARD my son complaining after he received his first paycheck: "Who is FICA, and why is 'he' taking so much of my paycheck?" Ahh, another adult entering the workforce and complaining about the government's take. Helping kids understand this very adult "thing" (taxes) is certainly imperative to their financial futures. As a financial advisor, I often observe how even my adult clients forget to account for taxes in their own planning. With adult clients, this "forgetfulness"—some might call it wishful thinking—usually comes in one of three flavors:

- They figure out their budgeting/spending based on their *gross* earnings, not the net they will receive after taxes. Obviously, our net income is the only portion of our earnings we are free to spend.

- When they look at their balance sheet, the amount they see in that vehicle that everyone urged them to invest in—the traditional 401(k)—isn't really the balance they will cash out with. They will still have to subtract taxes before getting their part.
- For those who don't have adequate withholding from their paychecks, they often get "shocked" with a huge tax bill in April because they under-withheld.

Once again, this is a lesson for kids that all adults can benefit from as well! When teaching your kids about taxes, I've found a logical order to help them really nail down the concept for the rest of their adulthood. Here are the two headlines that you'll want to cover:

1. What are taxes?
2. What types of taxes will I end up paying?

WHAT ARE TAXES?

Taxes are ways the government gathers money from its citizens to pay for items that we all use. For example, everyone in a town will have to pay for the schools, school buses, and textbooks. This applies even if those residents are elderly with grown kids, have no kids, or send their kids to private school.

As parents, we may be forever complaining about our taxes, but most of us understand "why" we pay them. Our complaints usually stem from how that money is being misspent. To a child, however, understanding why taxes need to be paid might not be initially intuitive, but it is easy to learn. And here is how to describe it to them:

First, you don't want to just jump right in and ask them: "Do you know what taxes are?" While I love directness, this is a topic requiring a slow build-up. Start by asking your kids about the last time they visited a local playground, beach, or national park; or used the library or the soccer field. Really let them build up the memory and share the experience with you about why they enjoyed their time there.

Then ask them: "What do you think are the costs that go into maintaining those places?" You can have a lot of fun with this one once you get past the obvious items. For example, in a school, the obvious items are things like books and computers. Depending on your child's age, they will likely be able to grasp that the teachers and administrators have salaries that someone has to pay. But what about the costs that go into running and maintaining the school? The heat/air conditioning, water, cleaning, painting, fixing the roof, mowing the lawn—the list could go on forever.

Now you get to the punchline. "Where does the money for all those things come from?" There is a chance that they don't know.

Finally, it might be fun to show them your town's budget. For example, I was easily able to go onto Google and search the budget of Anywhere USA—and lo and behold, it gave me this information which I printed out. Sometimes you can also find a fun color pie chart to show the kids. Here are a few of the items:

- Total Anywhere USA 2020 Budget: $210,000,000
    * Education: $128,000,000
    * Town: $76,000,000
        o Public Safety: $22,000,000
        o Parks and Recreation: $6,000,000
        o Public Works: $11,000,000
        o Human Services: $1,000,000
    * Other: $6,000,000

You can drive the point home in an age-appropriate contextual way to make sure the kids truly understand the concept by gamifying it for them. As you are driving around town, try to point things out and ask them, "Do taxes pay for that?" While their skate park and baseball field are financially supported by taxes, the local supermarket or McDonald's are not. Having said that, the supermarket and McDonald's certainly pay their fair share of taxes. Which leads us to the next level of discussion.

WHAT TYPES OF TAXES ARE THERE?

Taxes are collected in many ways including federal income tax, state sales tax, and local (town or city) tax on house and/or auto valuations. Businesses (like the McDonald's or supermarket in the previous example) also pay a complex series of taxes.

Below I have included the most common examples of taxes that your kids might be familiar with (or will have to get familiar with soon). I've also included what their rates might be in Connecticut, but you can easily find the information to adjust for your own state.

- INCOME TAX: You'll hear people complain about this kind of tax most often around April 15 when taxes are due on the prior year's income. This is the amount of money that comes out of each of your paychecks to cover the tax you owe at your tax rate. The more you make, the higher percentage rate you pay. This is a hard concept for kids to comprehend. Heck, it's a hard concept for some parents to understand. Nonetheless, you can give them the following example using a single filer since we are assuming that when our kids (or grandkids) enter the workforce, they will still be single:

* Tax Rate and Income Level

o 10% of the first $0–$9,700

o 12% of the amounts from $9,701–$39,475

o 22% of the amounts from $39,476–$84,200

o 24% of the amounts from $84,201–$160,725

o 32% of the amounts from $160,726–$204,100

o 35% of the amounts from $204,101–$510,300

o 37% of the amounts from $510,301+

* With high school students, you can take this one step further. Have them imagine that they are graduating from college with their first job. For argument's sake, let's say it pays them $40,000 annually. Which tax bracket would they fall into? And how much would they be left with after taxes? (Note: you can skip the lesson on effective tax rates here and give them a simple percentage to work with—unless you have a budding CPA on your hands.)

* Your child may be surprised that when they thought they would be earning $40,000, their take-home pay would only be $31,200. Those numbers look very different from each other. You can even help them set up an imaginary budget for when they are on their own (made even easier if they have participated in the family budgeting exercise in Lesson Three). What they can afford and what they will

have "leftover" looks very different before and after income tax. It is good for them to be prepared for this.

- SALES TAX: This is the amount of money that is tacked on to your purchases at the store. For example, in Connecticut the sales tax is 6.35%.
  * That means, if you buy an item at the store for $10, you will actually pay about $10.64 to walk out of the store with your purchase. If the item was $100, it would cost you $106.35. And if your purchase was $1,000, it would cost you $1,063.50. So it adds up, especially with the larger purchases.

- PROPERTY TAX: This tax is usually thought of as applying to homes, but it also applies to cars, boats, and a host of other things.
  * Home Property Tax: For an example, let's use a round number and say a home costs $500,000. Homeowners of the highest property taxes might pay a rate of 2%. That means, if you have a $500,000 property (I know that's a lot, but it's about doing easy math) you are paying $10,000 per year in taxes associated with that home.
  * For kids that are in high school, you might want to raise the level of the discussion by using property taxes. Ask them: "How is it determined how much we pay in property taxes every year?" Teach them that it all starts with the amount for which your house is assessed. You can have them go to Zillow and find out the approximate value of your house. (We know your town's assessed value, which can be found through your town's public records, is the final say on that value). Of course, you'll then tell them about mill rates which are the factor by which that home's assessment is used to determine the final property tax. A mill rate is equal to

$1 in taxes for every $1,000 in assessed value. To calculate your tax based on your mill rate, divide your assessed value by 1,000 and then multiply by your mill rate. For example, let's say a town has a mill rate of 17. For the above-mentioned home, you are dividing $500,000 by 1,000 to get $500, then multiply 500 by 17 (the mill rate in this example) to find that you are paying $8,500 annually in property taxes on a $500,000 property. That's a lot of money!

BONUS QUESTION

If you are a particularly brave parent, you may want to spark debate around this question: Is it fair for us to minimize the taxes we pay? This is akin to starting a conversation about politics or religion—lots of room for a heated discussion, that's for sure. Nonetheless, it is a good opportunity to teach ethics as well as local and national politics. If you can legally avoid paying some taxes, is it okay to do so? Should corporations be able to get a tax break because of the opportunities they provide for their employees to make their wages? I'm not going to try to give you any answers here, of course. I'm just saying that as adults we have had to face such questions. And that is our job as parents, right? To prepare our kids for the questions we know they will face.

For more information on this lesson, scan the QR code to visit our website.

LESSON EIGHT: EXPLAIN BORROWING AND CREDIT

Spending other people's money is fun ... until it's not.

As the English proverb goes: *"Loans and debts make worry and frets."*

As I mentioned in the introduction, it is crucial to develop financial literacy in our children if for no other reason than to help them have good physical and mental health during their adulthood. Show me an adult that didn't get off on the right foot financially, and I'll show you an overstressed individual that is either not in good health or heading for some health problems.

Debt often plays a huge part in that. People who tend to overextend carry the weight of the world on their shoulders as they worry over how they are going to get out of their predicament. But how did they get into debt in the first place?

My take is that no one ever sat them down to explain how borrowing and debt really works and how to navigate these financial tools in their lives. They probably didn't get the early lessons they needed to build a solid foundation before they started borrowing. If the credit card debt that we're seeing is any indication, it is a huge problem in our country.

U.S. consumers now owe nearly $1 trillion to credit card companies. Then there's the more than $1 trillion in outstanding student loans, widespread mortgage defaults, and so on. It's a problem whether viewed nationally—where we risk another economic meltdown by not addressing this issue head on—and personally, because this very real problem is coming to your family unless you cut it off at the pass.

Not all borrowing is bad. The purpose of this lesson is to help our children understand exactly what the short- and long-term implications are of borrowing, and how it might quickly turn into a long-term problem if they aren't careful. Credit, for example, has a way of providing instant gratification, which is not being helped by the social-media-based targeted advertising built into the smartphones our kids carry around. The urgency of discussing this topic cannot be overstated.

WHAT IS CREDIT?

To get started with our money conversation, we need to introduce a few terms to our kids, beginning with *credit*. Credit is the extent to which a person is trusted to make repayment of a loan. This is eventually reflected in someone's credit score, which is a numerical grade between 300 and 850; that number basically evaluates the likelihood that people will pay their bills. Kids may be fascinated to know that they will have their very own credit score someday, and that this score will determine whether they qualify for a loan, and at what interest rate, and with what credit limits.

Credit cards are a good way to improve a young adult's credit score by either making him or her an authorized user on your credit card, or, if they are at least 18 and have an income, to get their own credit card. They are also a good way (read: bad way) for all of us to get into serious trouble as credit cards make money easy to access but not so easy to pay back. This borrowing has its proper place in the management of money—you have the ability to buy something today, when you need it. However, you may end up paying for that item many times over if you get locked into a high interest rate (see below) and can only make your minimum payments.

Sometimes during one's college years they have their first experience with a credit card and don't quite grasp the problems they will incur should they not pay off that balance from month to month. It isn't uncommon to hear that they thought they only needed to pay the minimum—which we adults know is the path to financial ruin.

A few additional vocabulary words our kids need to understand regarding credit and borrowing:

- Borrower: This is the person who needs the loan. They are also called the debtor.
- Lender: This is the person with the money who makes the loan to the borrower. They are also called the creditor.
- Principal: The unpaid portion of a loan.
- Interest: An amount of money that's owed in addition to the amount borrowed. Interest is calculated on a percentage of the amount borrowed.

With these definitions in hand, you can discuss how a credit card that allows you 0% interest for an introductory period—and these offers will come to your kids, likely before they even leave for college—seems like a good idea, and they may be a good tool to pay other debt on a strictly time-limited basis. Nevertheless, no rate ever stays 0% forever. It can jump to 18%, 24%, or even as high as 30%, making it very difficult to pay off the principal.

Borrowing can be a good way to build up a credit history, which is something your child will certainly need in the future. In addition, using a credit card becomes a necessary next step on the road to buying more expensive items, such as a car and a home. But if they fail at the level of managing their credit card properly, that could do tremendous damage to their credit score which could prevent these larger purchases in the future. And while having poor credit might not prevent them from getting a loan, it will certainly cost them more in terms of higher interest rate costs.

This is why it's important that you build the fundamentals early on before they gravitate to a formal commercial credit card. Once they develop bad habits with a credit card, it is challenging to break them. Let's not even let it get to that point. The habits that are started in your kitchen, borrowing from the Bank of Mom & Dad, lay the groundwork. This is the first step in the evolution of their exposure to borrowing and as such is important and shouldn't be skipped. If they don't experience the early steps under your roof, you have left it to social media and advertising to get them off the right path.

THE BANK OF MOM & DAD

In our earlier discussions on allowance, I recommended not advancing money to your kids so that they could learn delayed gratification. That is, after all, one of the most important and long-lasting lessons of financial literacy. As they get a little older, however, you might be faced with the question of whether you want to sprinkle in a little experience with buying on credit.

In the early years, this didn't come in the form of a credit card but rather an IOU. You know the scenario. They have $10 saved up, and the object of their desire is $15. For some reason the purchase is time sensitive so you break down—even though you know you shouldn't give them an advance to teach them sound financial principles—and you make the executive decision to loan them the extra $5 now that they can pay back from their next allowance.

This seems fair assuming your child doesn't abuse their privileges by not doing their chores next week and bailing on giving you back your $5. As they get older, this issue will stick with you, and it is up to you to determine which borrowing opportunity calls for which response. By the way, saying "No" is an option, even though many parents have a tough time with that one.

There are some other good reasons to provide credit to your children which include:

- teaching them how it works;
- helping them start a small business (such as one that might require a loan to develop a website); and
- financing a car if you feel it is better that they drive themselves around than you continuing to be their personal Uber.

But just as often there are reasons not to provide credit in the form of a loan. Here are items you might include on your "No" list:

- You disapprove of your child's use of money. For example, if they want to get a motorcycle instead of a car right after passing their driver's license test, you might desire to put the kibosh on that.
- If you've lent money to them in the past, and they've somehow wriggled out of paying you back.
- If they make it a habit, so it is starting to become the norm and not the exception to their money management.
- Of course, if you can't afford it then this conversation is over. Don't worry, they'll figure it out.
- Family harmony—if lending to one child for the fourth time is going to seriously tick off another child, you've got to put some thought into that one.

Make it Formal

If you do decide this request for credit is a "Yes," it is important to take the time to sit down with your child to lay out the parameters on why you are allowing it, what the expectations are for paying back the loan, and the consequences if they don't follow the agreement.

Speaking of the word "agreement"... as I mentioned previously, it is a common teenager tactic to say some version of "You didn't say that" or "That's not what you told me." As formal as this may sound, if you are going to loan your child money, get it in writing. I have put an example on my website.

The following is basic information that can be included in this written agreement:

- The amount that is being borrowed (principal).
- Interest rate (applicable for use with older kids).
- Repayment terms (installments or lump sum on a certain date).
- What happens if the loan needs to be modified later. For example, they were sick for a week and couldn't do their chores for their allowance. Again, be careful here, this is for only very rare circumstances.
- Collateral for the loan in case they don't pay you back (might I suggest their smartphone—I know, I'm mean).
- Make sure they understand this is a loan, not a gift.
- Ask for their signature on the document (there's something about signing a piece of paper that makes almost all kids stand up a little straighter and take a situation more seriously).

Types of Borrowing

Once you've gone through the basics of borrowing and credit, and even experimented with a little home loan—at favorable terms—you can describe some other types of borrowing that they might encounter later in life. These could include:

- Personal Loans
- Auto Loans
- Student Loans
- Business Loans
- Mortgage (Home) Loans
- Home Equity Loans
- Credit Card Loans
- Loans from Friends/Family
- Payday Loans

This list really shows the importance that borrowing money plays in our financial system.

If you're really ambitious, you can also work in a conversation about the U.S. Debt. Not to be political, but our country doesn't set an amazing example for its citizens of how to balance a budget and keep its debt in check. If you want to show them something online that is very sobering, check this out:

https://usdebtclock.org/index.html?taxpayer=. How's that for an IOU?

For more information on this lesson, scan the QR code to visit our website.

LESSON NINE: INSPIRE THEM TO BE CHARITABLE

Many people are charitable to the extent that it doesn't cost them any money.

I THINK THOMAS JEFFERSON said it best when he proclaimed:

"I deem it the duty of every man to devote a certain portion of his income for charitable purposes; and that it is his further duty to see it so applied and to do the most good for which it is capable."

It is interesting that Jefferson not only advocates financial donations, with no strings attached, but he also encourages us to make sure that money is being spent wisely. It is that follow-through that cements the value of charity in a person's regular habits. And by a person, of course in the context of this book, I mean your child.

Helping your child understand the importance of charitable giving can be broken into a five-step process that involves giving away their money *and* their time, in the form of service. Both kinds of donations are valuable. They can be combined, or one can be chosen as more fitting to a particular circumstance. There are some adults who are more inclined to write a check whereas kids may feel they have more time than money to devote to a cause. But again, both are important, which is why they are both addressed below.

STEP 1: DEVELOP THE WHY

I don't know if you've ever talked to a teenager (sarcasm intended), but if you have, you have enjoyed (more sarcasm) their terse, one-word answers and willingness to shut you out. What this means is that they haven't matured yet to where they don't think that the sun, moon, and stars revolve around their own head. That's okay. In fact, you may not want to admit it, but we were the same way. Many of us were a bit self-absorbed, removed from the needs of others, and more obsessed with other things that didn't focus on those in need. But now look at how awesome we are.

Recognizing that you have your work cut out for you, you can start a discussion with one of those sullen adolescents by using a word they may not fully comprehend yet: philanthropy. Throw out that fancy word, with a smile on your face, and then tell them the definition.

Philanthropy: the desire to improve the well-being of humankind, as by charitable help or donations.

You can then ask them two follow-up questions:

"What do you think that means?"

Don't be in a rush to fill in the awkward silence after you ask them. Let them struggle a bit, maybe giving them a few hints. And remember, it doesn't matter what my view of philanthropy is, it matters only that you make it unique to your family's values.

Once you've gotten a sufficient answer, it's time to move onto the second question:

"Why do you think philanthropy is important for you, our family, and others?"

You might be surprised when the clouds of self-absorption break for a moment, and you are left looking at the beautiful light emanating from one of your own offspring as you share a bit of humanity. And then those clouds will roll right back in again.

STEP 2: TELL YOUR STORY

If you want to put a picture in someone's head, you have to tell them a story. In this case, you want to tell your kid a story from your own life about how you helped someone in need whether through giving money, acts of service, or both.

The story you choose needs to be one that they'll still remember 20 years down the road and may even repeat back to someone when you're not around.

As a financial advisor, I always know I've nailed it with a story I've told a client when they later remind me of something I had taught them. For example, when we were in the middle of a period where the stock market was booming, I was talking about asset allocation with a client. He interrupted me, almost mimicking me saying, "I know, I know, Tom. Never make a killing, never get killed … is why we diversify."

He may have thought he was teasing me, but I was beaming inside to think he remembered what I told him and was behaving in line with that mantra.

That's your goal. What's your personal story of being charitable? Who did you help? How? When? What was going on in your head? And most important, why did you choose to give?

Step 3: Help Them Make Their Own Story

It may seem like quite a leap from listening to the old codger, the parent, to getting your child off the sidelines and into the game of giving back. How the heck are we going to do this? If they were already charitable, we wouldn't even need this lesson plan, right? We need to focus on helping them develop their own story, something they can feel ownership in and be proud of.

Now that you have them in deep thought, tell them this:

> *"Tonight at dinner, we are all going to put together a list of charities or nonprofit organizations you'd like to help in some way. You have to be prepared to share some of your own ideas and also give a few supporting reasons."*

This encourages them to do a little research and dig into the areas of life that are important to them. Maybe it has to do with making sports equipment available to underprivileged areas. Maybe they are gravely concerned (although they would word it differently) about climate change. Whatever it is, invite them to tap their mind and heart. This is really one of those situations where there are no wrong answers.

Step 4: Choose a Set of Charities

After you've brainstormed during that dinnertime conversation, you are going to narrow down your efforts. At this point in your child's development, it is more important to go deep with a few charities than to cast too wide a net.

If you took my advice in Lesson One, your child will already have some money saved in their CHARITY jar. If they are older, this money may have been relocated to one of their bank accounts. You can donate that money progressively to build the feeling of giving throughout your child's young life.

In addition to that, you are now going to set up a family charitable fund. I'm going to use an arbitrary number to keep my math simple but don't get hung up on the exact amount. My wife, Stacey, and I have two children, so we are going to work with $800. This is the conversation we're going to have with our kids:

"As your parents, we feel like it's important to give to others. We want to encourage you to think about those in need and how you can make a difference—how we can make a difference. We've created a pot of money, $800, that we are going to dedicate to charity next year. Each of you can choose one organization from the list you created and give $100 from that fund to the charity of your choice. But in order to do this, you have to present to the family details about the charity, including how they use the money that comes in from donations. In addition to that, any money that you personally donate to that charity over the course of the year—from money you put aside from allowance, jobs, or even gifts from Grandma—we will match from that pot. For example, if you donate $10, we will add another $10 from the pot, making your donation $20. We will match any donation of yours up to $100."

There you go. You've incentivized them to think about good causes, others in need, and to take action. But wait, there's one more step. You are also going to do this as a family.

"We also think it would be fun to do this as a family. Of that $800, we are going to take the remaining half of the pot ($400) and use it for a charity that the four of us agree on together. It won't be the same as any of our individual charities. We are going to let you two kids meet separately and decide what that charity will be. Then you will run it by us for approval."

Now you are cooking. You've got them thinking of others, giving their own money, and having to work and dialogue with family members.

Sometimes these discussions can get heated when trying to come to a consensus, which is a good thing. Hint: unless they come back with the charity "Varsity Blues" (the college admissions scandal where parents fed money into a fake charity while the money was actually being used to falsify college applications) then let it go. If they agree on a charity, while it might not be your favorite organization, play for the greater good here.

STEP 5: DELIVERY OF THE GIFT

If possible, schedule a visit with your child to hand deliver the monetary gift. That will give them the additional picture in their mind of where the money is going. Especially with younger kids, the folks that work directly for these charities usually greet giving children with a huge smile and a ton of gratitude. Then your child gets to experience that feeling of accomplishment that only happens when we as human beings give to others.

If possible, take the hour to visit the charity's local chapter and then maybe celebrate with lunch afterward. Or even better, find an activity sponsored by that charity and have your child volunteer at the same time they are making their financial gift. Connecting physical actions with the donation of money can bring home the reality of helping others and deepens the joy they can experience by having an afternoon of selflessness. Afterward, they can go back to being the self-absorbed teenager we know and love—but I'll bet inside they are changed a little bit forever.

For more information on this lesson, scan the QR code to visit our website.

LESSON TEN: ADVISE THEM ABOUT INSURANCE

You pay now or you pay later. But you pay.

IN ITS SIMPLEST FORM, insurance is a vehicle we use to cover certain financial risks we have in our lives. Anything of value can be covered by insurance, so if it is damaged, lost, or stolen, you will be reimbursed for an agreed-upon amount by an insurance company. Of course, for this service you pay money known as a premium—and if nothing bad happens to whatever you are protecting, you don't get your money back. In that, it is a little bit like gambling, except that unlike gambling, you don't want to win, (i.e., have your property or health destroyed simply for a financial payout). On the contrary, if you take out insurance and don't ever need to use it, you have won—peace of mind. It's important to not underestimate the value of reducing the stress of worry.

We can get insurance on just about anything, nowadays. Here is a fun way to think about it by looking at some names that you may know. I have listed them in column A. Can you and your kids guess which body part listed in column B and insured amount in column C lines up with each of these famous people? (I have put the answers at the end of this lesson, so you are not tempted to cheat.)

Famous Person	Body Part	Amount Insured
America Ferrera	Legs	$27,000,000
Gene Simmons	Taste Buds	$1,000,000
David Beckham	Voice	$10,000,000
Fernando Alonso	Smile	$1,600,000
Bruce Springsteen	Teeth	$30,000,000
Angela Mount	Thumbs	$195,000,000
Julia Roberts	Whole Body	$31,200,000
Daniel Craig	Tongue	$9,500,000
Jennifer Lopez	Behind	$13,300,000

WHAT IS THE RISK?

Putting aside your individual answers to the quiz for the moment, why would someone insure any body part? They are seeking to mitigate risk. But what does "risk" really mean?

Simply put, risk is exposure to loss or injury. Some noninsurance ways we try to protect against risk are tactics like wearing a helmet when biking or having airbags in our cars. These are physical forms of insurance policies that acknowledge life has certain risks, and that we can cushion or otherwise deflect the negative effects of those risks.

Like you saw in the above chart, we can take out insurance for almost anything. During my 27+ year career in the financial services industry I've seen:

- Kidnapping Insurance—if you think there is a high ransom on your head. I once had a client ask me if there was some sort of insurance to try and get his son stolen instead of protecting against it. Obviously, he was joking … or maybe not.

- Fantasy Football Insurance—if a top pick gets injured and throws off your team (those leagues can be big business!)
- Bedbug Insurance—it actually costs a lot to get rid of these in your home.
- Chicken Insurance—which covers the bad behavior of your chickens.
- Cold Feet Insurance—in case someone doesn't go through with a wedding. I'm glad that wasn't an option back when I got married. My wife might have tried to collect on that one.
- Multiple Birth Insurance—as you can see in Lesson Two, "Teach Them the Value of a Dollar," having kids is expensive (estimated at over $250,000 per child). Imagine if, at the doctor's visit, they told you: "Congratulations! You are going to have a boy … and two girls. Yes, you're having triplets."

Since insurance can be perceived as a boring topic, I may have gone a little crazy thus far describing what you can insure. The fact is: Insurance is vitally important to any grown-up's financial plan. This means we have to find a way to package the conversation so that it's interesting as well as educational. Using the fun examples that we have gone through is a way to get the conversation started—they will help your child tune in, not out of the discussion.

Once you have their attention, you can help them understand that whenever we think *insurance,* we need to think *risk* at the same time. What is the risk of certain events occurring and how should that affect whether we take out an insurance policy—pay a premium—to protect ourselves in the face of them?

Think about the likelihood of these events, for example:

- Plane crash: 1 in 5,051.
- Shark attack: 1 in 50,453.

- Train crash: 1 in 156,169.
- Car accident: 1 in 84.

It is easy to see that insurance against a car accident would be of the utmost concern among the risks in this list.

MOST COMMON FORMS OF INSURANCE

Since, in reality, the list of potential losses is limitless, we as a society typically have insurance favorites that most diligent people include in their financial portfolio. There are two main buckets into which these common types of insurance fall: health-related items and property-related items.

Examples of health and welfare insurance coverages include:

- *Health/Medical Insurance*—covers medical expenses that arise due to an injury or illness. Typical expenses that are covered by health insurance include doctor's visits, hospitalization costs, medicine, and surgery. Typically, the insured/patient is responsible for some combination of a premium, copay, and deductible, and then the rest is covered by the insurance company. To help kids understand how crucial this form of insurance is, NerdWallet reported in 2018 that over 20% of adults in America struggled to pay their medical bills, and three in five bankruptcies were due to health bills.
- *Life Insurance*—a contract with an insurance company which commits that company to paying out a lump sum of money to an insured's beneficiary at death (death benefit) in return for premiums paid by the insured while they are alive. Typically, the beneficiaries of the policy use that money to pay expenses that would have otherwise been covered by the income of the person who died. Life insurance can be delicate to explain to a

child as having a parent who is no longer here to earn money is a tragedy. However, a parent who has not been prudent in preparing for this possibility is leaving their child with the possibility of double the tragedy.

- *Disability Insurance*—an insurance policy which promises to continue paying someone's wages if she or he becomes too sick or hurt to work at their job. The benefit payments, typically a percentage of one's monthly income, are paid after a stated waiting period, and last for a predetermined number of years (benefit period). This money is typically used to pay the insured's bills even though they are not earning money from their job. While most people imagine that disability will not happen to them, the statistics do not support this. A 35-year-old has a 50 percent chance of becoming disabled for a 90-day period or longer before age 65, while about one in seven people ages 35–65 can expect to become disabled for five years or longer.[6]

- *Long-Term Care Insurance*—this coverage typically helps older individuals with services that help for either a short or a long period of time. The services I am referring to help the individual live as independently and securely as possible when they can no longer perform everyday activities on their own such as: eating, bathing, dressing, toileting, transferring, and continence (also known as the six activities of daily living). This may be another category that is difficult to explain to our kids, but important nonetheless, not only from a financial perspective but also from an empathic one. And it is very common: 69% of Americans will need some form of Long-Term Care in their lives.[7]

---

[6]   https://www.affordableinsuranceprotection.com/disability_facts#:~:text=A%20 35%2Dyear%2Dold%20has,for%20five%20years%20or%20longer

[7]   https://acl.gov/ltc/basic-needs/how-much-care-will-you-need

Examples of property and casualty insurance coverages include:

1. *Automobile Insurance*—this protects the car owner from the costs due to an accident or theft. This would include protecting the property value and any liability that resulted from the accident.

2. *Renters/Homeowners Insurance*—this protects against losses and damages to an individual's home and the assets in that home. It might cover items such as interior damage, exterior damage, damage or theft of asset, and even injuries sustained by the family or others while in the home. To make the need for this insurance clearer, you can share these statistics with your kids: 5% of insured homes will have at least one claim each year, and 98% of those claims that are filed are due to property damage, including theft, with the average homeowners insurance claim amount being $12,474.[8] To bring that number even closer to home, see if you can compare that to an item that already exists in the household budget you put together in Lesson Two: "Teach Them the Value of a Dollar."

HOW INSURANCE WORKS IN PRACTICE

Now that we've gotten the right coverages in place, how does insurance work in practice? Basically, insurance provides protection against a loss by sharing that risk with others. In its most basic form, insurance is using small dollars so that you can protect against losing big dollars should you suffer a loss. By paying a small amount to the insurance carrier, you can pool that risk with others who are worried about the same thing. That pool of money is then used to compensate the few who will

---

[8] https://www.policygenius.com/homeowners-insurance/homeowners-insurance-statistics/

actually need it, and the insurance company gets to keep what is left over from that pool every year.

Each individual (or sometimes a company) enters into a contract between themselves and the insurance company specifying the coverage amounts, terms, and required premium to get that protection. It's important to teach kids that they need to read their coverages, so that their expectations will be met when it comes time to recoup their money. No one likes surprises.

The basic questions you need to think about as you spend your limited budget on insurance are:

- How much would I lose financially if this event happened?
- How much would it cost to insure against that loss?
- What is the probability of loss?
- Am I willing to accept the risk and not insure it?
- Will it provide me peace of mind to have this coverage?

Ah, that peace of mind I mentioned earlier in this lesson. Nothing beats it.

VOCABULARY KIDS SHOULD DEVELOP

Do you remember taking a foreign language in school? I remember one teacher who made us speak only Spanish when we were in her classroom. My confidence would be pretty high when I was talking with the other students … until they used a Spanish word that I didn't know. I would then get stuck in my brain trying to remember what the heck that word meant and would miss the next two or more sentences they said to me.

That happens all the time in our grown-up lives when we are talking about finance. Insurance is a foreign language to most people, and it helps if you have a good baseline of vocabulary, so your brain doesn't get stuck midconversation, especially if you are working with an insurance professional and learning about the coverage you're about to buy. We can give our kids a head start by helping them commit a few words to memory so that when they are part of an important part of a conversation later in life, these words ring a bell:

- Liability insurance: If you cause the accident, you are liable. That means you can get sued. If you have liability protection, that means you are protected if someone sues you.
- Deductible: The amount of money (or time) that you have to pay before the insurance company kicks in on their part.
- Policy: The formal agreement that binds the insurance company to doing what they said they were going to do. The policy specifically maps out what those coverages are.
- Benefit: The amount of money "the insurance company" will pay you if you suffer a loss from the risk they promised to cover.
- Premium: There is no such thing as a free lunch. The premium is what one pays to the insurance company so they can pool the risk and pay the people who put in a legitimate claim.

CONCLUSION

People typically obtain insurance when their potential loss is big. The motto to teach kids then is to insure the big things and self-insure the little things through a savings account or other emergency fund. In general, insurance is what you put in force to give you the combined benefit of financial protection and emotional comfort that the risks of life will not financially crush you. In life, there are usually two types of mistakes. Big mistakes which would include not insuring something that could financially disable you in a big way. Or little mistakes which, while annoying, aren't substantially financially life altering.

The most successful people I know make plenty of little mistakes but no big mistakes. The little mistake is paying a premium for coverage that you never put a claim in for. The big mistake is not paying for coverage which leads to financial ruin. Our kids will get to make their choices someday, and we will want them to make the right ones.

And now, here is the answer key to the quiz I gave you at the beginning of this chapter. I wonder how many you got right?

ANSWERS		
Famous Person	**Body Part**	**Amount Insured**
America Ferrera	Teeth	$10,000,000
Gene Simmons	Tongue	$1,000,000
David Beckham	Legs	$195,000,000
Fernando Alonso	Thumbs	$1,000,000
Bruce Springsteen	Voice	$31,200,000
Angela Mount	Taste Buds	$16,000,000
Julia Roberts	Smile	$30,000,000
Daniel Craig	Whole Body	$9,500,000
Jennifer Lopez	Behind	$27,000,000

https://www.bemoneyaware.com/blog/insurance-of-celebrities-body-parts-hollywood-and-bollywood/

For more information on this lesson, scan the QR code to visit our website.

Lesson Eleven: Demystify Legal Documents

Either you or the State can decide where your money goes.

Many parents don't feel comfortable putting the topic of legal documents, such as wills and health-care proxies, on the to-do list of financial concepts to teach their children. They might say, *Well, I don't think that's really relevant.* I think I understand the real reason why we avoid these conversations. Families are fighting enough negativity that is brought into our households from the media (remember, "if it bleeds, it leads") and adding legal documents that presuppose the worst-case scenario to that list of downer conversations just doesn't feel like a good use of time.

And yet—and you know there was a yet coming—it is that exact tendency to avoid the conversation that will cause your kids to take a piece of irresponsible financial planning with them into adulthood and likely even pass that on to their families as well.

As an advisor, I spent the good part of my career with new clients coming into my office for their initial consultation, typically married couples with young kids, only to find that they hadn't yet had a will drafted. In my earlier years, I was pretty judgmental, thinking to myself: *How could you have young kids and not take the time to at least set up some basic estate planning that named guardians for them should something happen to you?*

As time went on and I matured as a financial planner and as an adult, I came to understand that this wasn't a decision these young parents were consciously making. The issue stems from them not getting a proper education themselves when they were younger. If they were not taught to understand the importance of these legal documents and the emotional devastation that can occur when this side of their planning was left unattended, how would they know to do anything differently when they came of age?

We can stop that trend. Having this conversation at your dinner table puts the concepts of these legal documents in your children's heads and makes them a part of their future planning. In fact, they are going to need to do some planning involving these documents starting from when they are as young as 18 years old. Stay tuned for that, later in the chapter.

Of course, there is another reason this topic may be labeled taboo in your house. And that is, you are embarrassed that you haven't yet done your own wills and "what if" documents. As I have said before, we don't have to let our own incompleteness cause us to avoid a conversation. Rather, you can use this as a way to be vulnerable in front of your kids. Tell them you are embarrassed that you haven't yet attended to these parts of your own planning, but that they are important, and you are using this conversation with them to hold you accountable to getting that done. It will turn out to be a fantastic conversation about family values—what is important to you as an adult and what you wish for them even if you aren't here to carry it out. These are the emotional conversations parents dream of having with their kids—and now you have the catalyst to chat about it.

As a bonus, if you've been carrying a nagging, bad feeling around for years that you haven't done this planning, it is almost guaranteed that once you get this part of your life in order you will say to yourself: "Wow, that wasn't hard at all. I feel so much better now. Had I only gotten it done earlier, I wouldn't have had to stress about it over all these years." I have never had a client say to me: "Tom, I feel worse now that I've checked estate planning documents off my list of to-dos." Never once. And I'm betting I'll never hear it.

WHY DO FAMILIES NEED LEGAL DOCS?

I always find it helpful when you kick off this conversation with the "why." Why do families need to focus on legal documents? You can use any form of this metaphor that works for you:

- You need to pack your parachute before you jump out of the plane.
- You want to put on your life preserver before you get knocked off the boat.
- You will need to have insurance before the fender bender, not after it has already happened.

We could keep going but any one of these will get the point across. Estate and "what if" documents become useful, if not necessary, at the worst of times. As far as what constitutes the worst of times, well, I think the whole family should be sitting down for the discomfort of what comes next. They come into play when someone:

- dies;
- has a tragic accident that they don't die from but that leaves them in a medical emergency—the worst of which could be that they are put on life-support systems; or
- deals with the medical treatment for someone else who can't make decisions on their own.

If you're like me, just reading that makes you feel queasy. But here is the reality. If those things are going on in someone's world, does it make sense to compound the emotion and stress by having a legal wrangling because none of the decision-making was made before it happened? Families in these tragic situations now have the compounded stress of a tough conversation of deciding which medical treatment you would have wanted to have or how you would have wanted your estate distributed, in addition to the grief and confusion they are feeling (and possibly some intrafamily squabbles as well). Wouldn't you rather that your family had as easy a road as possible when dealing with these dire circumstances?

I'm sure this resonates with you. If you are parents who are concerned enough to want to teach your child about money and give them a solid foundation on which to build as they go out into the world, you are the same type of parents who want to make responsible decisions in your own planning with the end goal of taking care of your family—not only financially, but also emotionally.

At the end of the day, the legal documents we're about to discuss force families to have tough conversations when emotions are calm, and everyone can think clearly. The time to have those conversations is never when the chaos of the event erupts. When you plan for the inevitable "what ifs," it gives you an immediate plan of action when no one is anywhere near their best.

LEGAL DOCUMENTS FOR A GOOD PLAN

Now that you've been inspired to complete your own planning, let's turn our attention to how to prepare your kids for the inevitable decisions they'll have to make, with some of those actions coming as early as 18 years old. Here is the short list of legal documents they'll want to have and what each one is for.

Wills

A will is a legal document that lays out how a person wishes their property to be distributed after their death. It sets forth where you intend certain property and assets to go and who is in charge of making sure that happens.

There are a few vocabulary words that will be helpful for your children to know and will make it easier for you to describe what a will is. They include:

- Decedent: the deceased.
- Beneficiary: anyone receiving a gift or benefiting from what's being left by the decedent.
- Executor or Administrator: the person appointed by the decedent to make sure their assets get distributed in the way the decedent specified in his or her will.

Here is the short explanation of a will for you to share with your child: People set up a will so when they die (which we all do at some point) and become the "decedent", the "executor" will know who will be the "beneficiary" of each of the items the decedent owned before he or she died.

In other words, a will identifies where my stuff is going and who is going to help get there.

There is one other nuance that you might want to bring up here, but doing so will add to additional complexity to the conversation. It's about guardians and trustees. I'll only need to define these terms for you to understand the sensitivity of this part:

- Guardian: who will take care of minor children if you die.
- Trustee: who will take care of the money for a minor child if you die.

You can see why this subject would be challenging as your kids might have their own feelings about who the person is that they would be living with should something happen to you. What they deem to be the best decision might not be how you feel about it based on the vantage point you have of the child, the guardian, and your life experiences. I think it's an amazing conversation to have, but it does come with a bit of potential conflict which is beyond the point of my efforts here.

Health Care Proxies

A health care proxy is a legal instrument where individuals name a person who becomes responsible for making health-care decisions on behalf of them (as patients) when they are incapable of making these medical decisions on their own. When a set of circumstances brings you to this point, the document "springs" into action and allows the appointed person to step in and guide the way. It is the health-care version of a durable power of attorney (and sometimes referred to as a "durable medical power of attorney"), which we will discuss further below.

Basically, this instrument gives a third party the legal authority to act on behalf of the patient, in conjunction with the patient's health care team when the patient is not capable of making those decisions for himself/herself.

I promised you that I'd get to this important point. Once your child has reached 18, they need to execute a health care proxy too. These documents are used in situations where your 18-year-old is unable to make decisions regarding their own health care. Over my many years as a financial planner, I've seen hundreds of times where parents of children who are leaving to go to college either completely forget, or scramble at the last minute, to have this important document signed by their now freshman year college student. Imagine the problems that could arise should there be a "what if" and you are hundreds of miles away.

Power of Attorney (POA)

This is a document which gives one person the power to act for another person. For example, in our household, my power of attorney document gives another the power (the agent) to act on financial decisions about things like my property or finances. A "General Power of Attorney" covers legal, financial, and business matters.

When these documents are created, they are either broad or limited in their authority, based on one's comfort level and specific situation. You might have used such a document in the past, for example at a real estate closing where a spouse can't be present to sign the documents necessary to complete the transaction. I would highly recommend that if you (the parent) have used such a document in the past, that you tell your kid(s) the story about it during this dinner conversation. It will help the concept stick in their head.

Typically, these POAs last until the principal person revokes the POA, dies or gets divorced (if the spouse is named as the agent). Also, if the agent is no longer able to carry out the tasks required with that power, their authority can end.

Some people don't feel at all comfortable with giving anyone a blanket power of attorney. In those cases, they might choose to use what's called a "springing" POA, which only goes into effect when the primary person is incapacitated. POAs do not pertain to some medical decisions, so let's talk about that.

Living Wills

This may be the most difficult document to talk about, so I'll be short and sweet, and you can feel free to be the same with your kids. Some parents choose to leave it out entirely; it is of course up to you what and how much to teach your kids and at what age. If you do want to include it in the conversation, here's what you might consider covering with your child.

A living will is a legal document that lays out what medical treatments you would, and would not, want to use in keeping you alive if it came to that point. It allows you to express your wishes regarding end-of-life treatment if the time comes and you are unable to relay your preferences. As you'll experience, this conversation has 90% to do with your values. Basically, you have to determine, before you get to this terrible point, what circumstance might make life not worth living.

This document, which may be a simple "check the box" type of form, will address a large number of possible end-of-life decisions at a time where you might not be "of sound mind and body" to articulate them to the medical staff. And remember, the medical staff's job is to keep you alive, and without your directive, that's exactly what they will do.

Here is a very short list of items that are typically addressed in a living will:

- Mechanical ventilation.
- Tube feeding.
- Antibiotic medications.
- Pain management.

Additionally, these documents typically mention organ donations and are often combined with health care proxies. And with that said, I don't think we need to dive any deeper into those examples.

Trusts

I saved this one for last as the mention of trusts unfairly brings up visions of complexity and makes people feel that using them is only an issue for the very wealthy. While that's not entirely accurate, I understand that the media and television have made people feel this way. Let's have a quick chat about this one with your kids.

When an individual sets up a trust, they are creating a legal entity where the owner gifts specific property to another person (trustee) who must look after it and use it, for the benefit of a third party. Basically, we are trusting someone to look after some money or asset (like property) for someone else. This could be a parent who sets aside money for their five-year-old son, Spencer, where Aunt Mary Beth (trustee) is in charge of investing the money and distributing it to or for Spencer's benefit. Often, trusts specify an age where the beneficiary is able to take over complete control of the trust assets without needing to go through the trustee. For example, the trust might say: "When Spencer reaches age 30, the trustee is directed to distribute all of the trust property to Spencer outright and free of trust."

The reason that people typically associate trusts with wealthy individuals is not a completely unfair pairing. There are many strategic uses of trusts that outweigh the sometimes lofty costs of establishing and administering them. For example, trusts may offer tax minimization, creditor protection, and reassurance that money eventually gets to the intended beneficiaries without potential legal battles from other disgruntled family members.

CONCLUSION

This might be the most difficult of our dinner conversations. It's dicey, I get it. But think about what it does for your child. First, it basically makes any topic fair grounds to talk about in the house. Heck, you talked about dying, being disabled, and all sorts of other gruesome potential things that can happen. Talking about underage drinking seems like a piece of cake compared to these topics.

Second, it plants the seed in their heads that: Being a responsible adult includes taking the time to think through these uncomfortable conversations and taking actions to prepare for them should they happen.

And finally, you might even get some insight about how they feel about things as they pertain to your personal family's situation. Maybe you didn't know that they really, really, really didn't like the person you planned to make the guardian of them should something happen to you.

Yes, these are not easy conversations. But maybe it's time to make difficult conversations not taboo in your household.

For more information on this lesson, scan the QR code to visit our website.

LESSON TWELVE: WARN THEM ABOUT MONEY SAFETY

If your accounts were meant to be shared,
they wouldn't ask for a password.

IT WAS BENJAMIN FRANKLIN WHO coined the phrase: "An ounce of prevention is worth a pound of cure."

When it comes to safeguarding your assets and reputation, that is great advice. We work so hard to build our financial futures and relationships, yet it is easier than you think for all of that to be thrown into disarray in today's cyberworld.

Building good habits that protect your identity and net worth can start at a young age. And while the techniques that the world's unsavory characters use to steal will change, the idea that you are putting your family's security front of mind by taking the necessary extra steps can be modeled to your kids.

The following is a list of items to cover with your child this month to get them thinking about the subject and what kind of precautions can be taken. I'll bet they can even come up with other ideas that we haven't thought of yet! And if they do, be sure and share them with Total Cents so it will benefit other families as well.

Using Paper

A study released by the Better Business Bureau reminded us that a fair amount of identity crime occurs from paper-based channels. Some of this comes from stolen paper (either through the trash or even your mailbox) or the worst—when you lose your wallet.

You'll find these numbers interesting. Studies show that people who monitor their accounts online incur an average loss of $551, while the average loss when detected from paper statements is a whopping $4,543.

After sharing those staggering numbers, ask your kids: "What can our family do to protect against fraud from paper statements?" This might feel like a "duh" question, but it is a great one to warm up the entire security conversation. Here are some of the answers you might hear from your kids (or supply to them when they've exhausted their ideas):

- Replace paper bills with electronic versions.
- Pay your bills online, electronically.
- Shred, shred, shred!
- Sign up for auto-deposits.
- Be militant about getting to your mailbox. And if you're going away, stop the mail for the time you'll be gone.
- Don't keep all your passwords on a piece of paper in your wallet—or anywhere on paper, for that matter. Our family uses an Excel spreadsheet which is password protected, and then I keep that document in a second secure area. If the criminal gets to that sheet, they deserve to have all my money.
- If you have to use paper, keep an eye open for when items such as your credit card statement go missing.

- There are also many services out there which I haven't personally used, such as LastPass, 1Password, and Keeper which attempt to accomplish a similar way of storing passwords.

Protecting your Social Security Number

Many think that the reason Social Security numbers were invented was to establish a national identification for Americans. Actually, during the development of the Social Security Act of 1935, it was economist Edwin Witte who came up with the idea of using them to track the new retirement payment system. The number's sole purpose at the time was to track one's earning histories for use in the determination of retirement benefit levels.

Obviously, it has many more uses today, and common forms of identity theft start with obtaining your Social Security number. That leads to all sorts of access and fraudulent account openings as well as a host of other crimes. With your Social Security number, new credit cards can be applied for, tax refunds can be redirected—the list is nearly endless. And all of these can have disastrous effects to your credit score (discussed in Lesson Eight).

Ask your kids: "How can we avoid this from happening?" Some common responses may include:

- Memorize your Social Security number instead of needing to carry around the Social Security card itself.
- While you're at it, keep that card in a very safe place (see my thoughts about paper above).
- Be very guarded about sharing that number. When in doubt, ask, "Why do you need that?" While a bank or investment company might, in fact, need it, the fast-food delivery people don't. And if they insist, pick another place to do business.

This can lead to uncomfortable conversations with some of your service providers. But you'd rather have that uncomfortable conversation as opposed to trying to clean up identity fraud. Remember what Benjamin Franklin said at the beginning of this lesson and take the side of the ounce of prevention.

Using Hard Currency

Is it even worth it to teach our kids about managing actual money? Yes, I'm talking about paper currency and coins. Will this next generation even use that? While I'm not 100% confident they will be 10 years from now, I do want to talk about it a little since we are still using it today. The safety and security components of this subject include:

- visits to a bank's ATM; and
- where to keep money when traveling (including traveling abroad).

Let's start with visits to the bank's ATM. I can't have been the first person to have wondered, at some point, if a robber was going to come up behind me and steal all my money.

This becomes more unlikely, however, if you carefully choose which ATM locations you get money from, and keep in mind some practical things, such as:

- being aware of your surroundings;
- locking your doors at drive-thru ATMs;
- not counting your money in front of the ATM; and, of course,
- if someone attempts to rob you, just give them the money. My mother always warned me: "Things can be replaced. People can't."

A far more common risk at the ATMs, however, revolves around identity theft. At an ATM, it is crucial not to let anyone see your PIN (and certainly don't share it with anyone) and to watch out for card skimmers (devices that criminals attach to ATMs, gas pumps, and any other payment terminals to steal your card's information).

Carrying Physical Money

Another aspect of this discussion topic is where to keep physical money. I like to frame this question in the context of traveling abroad or far from home as I think that is when people would worry the most (or begin to worry at all).

My generation was big on using traveler's checks, but that form of carrying money has seen less use over the years. Instead, we're starting to see much more use of prepaid travel cards as a safe and popular way by which travelers carry money abroad. This card is often loaded in multiple currencies, which certainly comes in handy.

As to how to carry that paper currency, here are a few strategies that your children might come up with (well, maybe after a little prompting by you):

- Split up your money and store it in different areas.
- Hide your money using:
    * Money belts
    * Money socks
    * Pocket underwear—yes, a money bra is available too

SOCIAL MEDIA

Guarding your financial safety on social media is a new frontier for all of us, not just our kids. Some aspects of our discussion with them might include these examples:

- Set strong passwords. The passwords shouldn't be easy to guess, should have a mix of character types, and should be fairly long.

I'm not a tech guru, but I try to have mine be at least 10–12 characters long.

- Don't post sensitive information including financial account information or photo IDs on social media (do I even need to tell anyone that?). And whatever you do, don't post about the great 2-week vacation you are on—that is asking for trouble. You don't want to announce to the world that you won't be at your home for a couple of weeks. That is an invitation to anyone who needs anything to walk right in and take it.
- Finally, monitor your security settings for each social media platform you use including:
  * Use different passwords for each platform.
  * Change your passwords every few months.
  * Two-step authentication wouldn't hurt either. This is an extra layer of security you add to your account in case your password is stolen.
  * Don't post about expensive purchases you have made lately.

And while you're at it, discuss with them about not posting things that will prevent them from getting into a college or getting a good job.

Talking About Money Publicly

I could write another book about this one topic. As a financial advisor, I forged amazing relationships with my clients because I was practically the only one outside of their family that they openly discussed money with.

While the theme of Total Cents is not making money a taboo topic in your own house, I would say it's quite all right to make it a taboo topic in social circles. Can you imagine someone at a party asking you:

"How much money did you make last year?" Or, "How much inheritance money did your parents leave you?"

Not everyone agrees with me, but many do. A survey conducted by Ally Bank showed that 70% of Americans think that it's rude to talk about money. I must say I wholeheartedly agree that talking about money publicly in this fashion is inappropriate to the point of crass. Share with your child that there is no reason to do it. It's not anyone's business. Not to mention most people will view you as a social pariah if you make a habit of inappropriately talking about money in a social setting.

My bottom-line advice: DO talk about money in your home. DON'T talk about your personal detailed financial situation in social settings.

READING THE FINE PRINT

Because of some situations I became aware of in my career, I've tried to teach my kids to not sign things without reading them. However, I completely understand how today's compliance-filled legal society has us just clicking "I agree" as you'd never get to the rest of your day if you actually read through all these things. This is a matter of personal frustration for me that we've made things so hard for normal consumers to do the right thing and read what they are signing because of the legalese of it all.

I will admit that I have gotten caught in some of those introductory free offers that then switches over after 3 months to a paid subscription. I always find those impossible to figure out how to unsubscribe.

It's important to know what you are signing up for. Whether it be understanding what an insurance policy will and won't cover, or what fees a credit card will charge under certain circumstances, it's important to burn into our kids' brains that knowing this information *before* they commit is important.

Making Loans to Friends

When I caution people about making loans to friends, there are often those who take issue with it. I completely understand why they might feel that way. I certainly have tremendous gratitude for my financial stability and understand the feeling that I should share with those in my circle who are less fortunate.

Of course, there is a "but." Over the years, I have watched clients with money get approached by a friend or family member for a loan. More often than not, it was because the friend or family member hit a rough patch. It is certainly natural to be sympathetic to these situations.

I have also seen good relationships deteriorate when financial loans take place between family members or close friends for any number of reasons:

- The borrower feels embarrassed and thus, after the loan is made, they avoid interactions with their lending friend because of self-imposed (and often imagined) shame that is attached to their needing money.
- The lender watches the borrower spend money on what they deem to be frivolous things, which leads to feelings of resentment that they're not paying back the loan. This can put an awful strain on a relationship.
- Sometimes the lender feels some entitlement for something because they bailed out the borrower. Maybe that is warranted, but some take it too far.

I could go on, but my advice stands: Avoid lending to family members or close friends if you can help it. A client once told me that they gifted the money to a friend as they wanted to avoid all the mentioned pitfalls. I thought that was a great way to think, but the skeptical side of me wonders if they were calling it a gift but, in the back of their mind, they really had some attachment—the entitlement I spoke of—as if it were a loan.

In closing, all of the items mentioned in this lesson could be modified, have counterpoints, and can be argued. Nonetheless, I think it's important that you bring these topics up at your dinnertime conversation to put it front of mind. How one chooses to think about it or which tactics to use to protect yourself is a personal choice. All I'm asking is that you and your kids talk about it.

For more information on this lesson, scan the QR code to visit our website.

CONCLUSION

You did it. You bought this book and took my advice to have these conversations, one after another, while not worrying about how you looked during it. "The journey of a million miles begins with the first step." Well, you took the first step by reading this book and having one dinner conversation per month.

My best advice to you is—don't stop. Keep it going. You are having great conversations with your kids on topics they find interesting, in part because they are interesting and in part because you are making them so. Deep down, kids—yes, even those surly teenagers—want to spend time learning from their parents. Equipping them for their lives ahead makes them feel close to you. Just don't expect them to tell you that or thank you.

What your kids don't realize is that your prioritization of these subjects is going to give them a leg up in the "real world." I would challenge you then to continue to look at the content on www.totalcents.com and use that as fodder for future conversations. Read the parent-appropriate information we continue to put out and then be sure to forward the social media teen info to your kids to keep their interest piqued (not to mention those social media algorithms going).

Why shouldn't you stop now? For the same reason that you don't slip back into eating donuts and laying around on the couch all day after resetting your diet and exercise routine and finally hitting your weight goal. Just as incremental improvements and continued maintenance help keep our physical bodies in shape, continually refreshing these financial concepts keeps your child fluent in financial literacy.

Once you have laid these cornerstones of discussion and understanding, you will also be more prepared for things that you'll see on the road ahead. The financial topics don't necessarily change as our kids get older, but the context for a college student and then young adult in the workforce changes a bit. You will want to be aware of what's coming next so you can gently and gradually prepare your son/daughter for what's coming and what their responsibility will be at that time. Basically, we need to wean them off of their need for us so they can lean on themselves more and more.

That may be hard to hear as a parent; we always want to feel important to our kids. I'm not asking you to stop having that very natural desire to be needed. Rather, I am suggesting that you evolve the things they need you for. After all, it's our job, as parents, to make our kids self-sufficient.

WHAT TO EXPECT IN COLLEGE

Now that your kids have a good foundation of financial knowledge, we want to let them practice so they can attain mastery. And here's how we can do this—remember, slow and steady wins the race.

Your kids will need money in college. Obviously, there are the expenses of tuition, room, and board. Many parents attempt to cover those items for their children, but on top of that there are other random expenses that come up. You've had the conversation on budgeting, so they understand the gist of this topic. You'll want to be clear as to what you, the parent, will cover and what they will be expected to cover, either through work-study, other in-term employment, or savings from summer jobs. I would suggest that the amount you give them as their monthly allotment be small enough that they still have some wants. And with that they will be forced to make some money that they can use to supplement your allotment for things they'd like to spend money on.

Given those parameters, here's how you might think about developing their financial literacy during college. The goal is to help them develop good budgeting habits over the next four years. Figure out how much you would like to supplement your college student's spending money on a weekly basis. You might start their freshman year by transferring this spending money from your bank account to the student's. (I would suggest Mondays so they don't get the money on a Friday and blow through it on a weekend binge!)

Then, in their sophomore year, fund their spending money at the same level (or perhaps their literacy has grown to the point that they request a small bump for inflation!) but transfer the money into their account every 2 weeks. That forces them to stretch out their money so it lasts a bit longer. In their junior year, change the frequency to monthly. And I bet you can guess where I'm going with this. During their senior year, give them a lump sum at the beginning of the semester. This process will result in a slow build toward good habits that allows them to make mistakes early on, which aren't as painful. And remember, whenever they come up short—let them deal with it. Don't bail them out. If you do, you'll be bailing them out the rest of their lives.

WHAT TO EXPECT IN THE WORKFORCE

Congratulations! Your kids are launched. They have secured their first job, their first apartment, and now they get to put all these great money lessons to work in the real world. It's very important that you have a dinner with them at the end of their senior college year to give them the heads-up of what's ahead.

Key topics you might include in that conversation are:

- Retirement Plan Savings—We have talked a lot in this book about the importance of saving. Time to give them a reminder. They must understand that enrolling in this plan is mission critical. Remember that doing something beats doing nothing. But doing the maximum contribution allowed under the plan is the best. The middle ground is for them to at least contribute an amount that maximizes any company match that might be offered. These programs allow them to automate the "pay yourself first" or "save first, then spend" habit. Along with their contributions, you can talk about how to invest that money. Retirement plans have a longer time horizon that lend themselves to investors who tend to be more aggressive with their investment choices. These plans make it easy to figure out what that asset allocation should be. Many have questionnaires that you can complete which then lead to various funds that fit a particular goal.

- Disability Insurance—Once your kids have something to protect, namely, their income, it is time to discuss this type of insurance. If you calculate what those earnings will potentially be over their 40+ years of working, it is a big number and is worth protecting. They need to know that it is their responsibility, not yours. If they suffer a disability which causes them to stop being able to work and earn that is their financial problem—and they need to spend a couple of bucks to protect that.

- Health Insurance—Doctor visits are expensive, and when they have a problem, it can get really expensive. And those doctor bills don't disappear because they don't have the money to pay them. If they don't have the money to cover it, they either won't get treatment or it will lie on the shoulders of the

Bank of Mom/Dad. They can't put themselves in that situation—and shouldn't put you in that situation. Many parents choose to continue keeping their younger adult children on their health insurance plans for a few years after college, but this perk will disappear eventually. And it should! By the way, we didn't discuss Health Savings Accounts (HSAs) in this book, but they should start one of these too. We'll save that for the next book.

- Legal Coverage—Many benefits plans are now offering a prepaid legal option. You never know what you're going to need legal advice for as we talked about in the last lesson. It could be as easy for your adult child as getting a simple will or those "what if" documents. Enrolling in a plan lets them, fairly inexpensively, check a few grown-up documents off their to-do list as well as prepare for that event that they didn't see coming.

HOW DO YOU KNOW IF YOU'VE WON

I thought long and hard about whether or not to use the phrase "won" when it comes to parenting. I tried to figure out if I'd be offending anyone implying that there are winners and losers in parenting.

Deep down we would all prefer to be considered a winner. And for a parent, being a winner means we have raised well-adjusted, resilient kids who are prepared to handle whatever life throws at them. Specifically, winning in raising a financially literate child looks like this:

- They feel a level of comfort in coming to you to talk about money issues. They know you might not have the answer but are open and receptive to the conversation.
- They have taken on the financial attitude of: "If it is to be, it's up to me." They aren't looking for a handout from you. They

have the confidence to know they can do it, and the pride to do it themselves.

- They understand that, as it pertains to their financial future 30 years down the line, there is a sense of urgency to start right away. Procrastination is not their friend in this area of their lives.
- They feel comfortable seeing things about social media and knowing which of it is BS and what is helpful to look at. Meaning, they don't get caught up with "keeping up with the Joneses."
- They have a deep sense of responsibility for planning for a rainy day. That includes emergency reserve funds, asset allocation, insurance protections, and legal documents.
- They have enjoyed the learning process and have vowed to make sure they have the same conversations when they become parents.
- They trust in the financial planning process and don't let the bumps in the road throw them off course, or create worry, which can eventually lead to adverse health consequences.
- They are clear that money decisions are never perfect, but the law of large numbers shows that the more financial decisions they make which are at least in the ballpark of being right, the better the aggregate of their outcomes will be.

That's what makes you a successful parent when it comes to raising a money-smart kid. And by the way, opening the conversations about money has a high correlation to them inviting you into other nonmoney conversations in their lives. Ultimately, you want to be useful, and our kids have a lot of needy moments when they will appreciate having your ear. Be that parent that they are depending on you to be. You can do it!

About the Author

Tom Henske has been a leader in the financial industry for nearly three decades. Tom started his career in financial planning in 1994, with Cowan Financial Group. Shortly thereafter, he started his own company, Henske Advisors. In 2003, they were acquired by National Financial Partners (merging them into Lenox Advisors) which went public shortly thereafter. Tom remained an equity partner until 2020 when he retired to focus solely on matters of life insurance and building Total Cents.

While the seven financial professional designations after his name demonstrate his qualifications, it is his 11 years of coaching high school varsity soccer and the parenting of his two teenage children that have made him the real expert. A two-time All-American and three-time NCAA Division I Soccer Champion for the University of Virginia Cavaliers, Tom has again found victory in his mission to provide a better way for parents to develop a generation of money-smart kids. He invites you to join him on the journey.

Made in the USA
Middletown, DE
04 March 2023

26211814R00076